On the Road for Travelball

A Parent's Guide to
Traveling the Travel Team Circuit
without *Constantly* Blowing a Circuit

SUE ROSENFELD

LIGHT YEAR
PRESS

Contents

Introduction

L ike a baseball game that goes into extra innings, highlights and surprises characterized our family's first travel team experience. When we started with travel teams, we'd been on the baseball journey for many years. That first travel year involved both a summer travel team and a high school team that traveled. I learned a lot from other parents as I observed, chatted, and asked questions. But I didn't always know what questions to ask or who to ask. And while there were days of lush, beautiful terrain, there were also days that felt like being on a narrow, zigzagged road, a rugged mountain trail, or a dusty path.

Are you in the middle of your first travel team experience? Is a travel team on the horizon for you? Does this year mark a decade of travel sports for your family? Whether you're looking for answers to unspoken questions, ideas to make the experience even better, ways to adjust after a tough season, or just intrigued by the book's title: Welcome!

Here you'll find ideas and fun about a journey that can be easily swallowed up by tiring logistics or become focused solely on wins and losses. Blank pages at the end of each section in the book give you space to record fun memories of your family's travel days and create a treasure to pass on to generations. But most of all, let what you find on the pages of this book encourage your heart, mind, and soul to have endurance and perseverance for a special time in your family's life—the imperfect adventure of travel sports.

With intention, this imperfect adventure can be full of enjoyable moments. With intention, wins and losses can be a partner with discovery and fun. With intention, you can manage logistics without continually feeling overwhelmed. And that's the essence of this book: peace in logistics, joy in creating, and beauty in moments. Since we were involved in travel baseball, that is the backdrop of the book. Other sports are woven throughout in various ways, including anecdotes from parents whose family traveled for sports in addition to or instead of baseball. From one traveler to another, it is possible to travel the travel team circuit without *constantly* blowing a circuit!

—Sue

PART I
Taking Time for a Family Huddle—
Before It's an Emergency

I looked out the window and spotted my son in a car I didn't recognize. An impromptu outing for the players was in the works, but I didn't know it when I glanced up from my computer as I worked in the hotel lobby. With a rush of adrenalin quickening my steps, it didn't take long to cross the lobby and get outside to the car. My pounding heartbeat eventually subsided as I recognized the drivers and passengers, learned the outing details, and got a parent's cell phone number.

I realized then that my husband and I had neglected one important thing with our son before embarking on an out-of-state tournament with a new team—a huddle to establish a framework for the trip and to discuss communication logistics. Later that day, the three of us did have a huddle. And while the learning curve wasn't steep that time and the adjustments minor, the confusion could have been alleviated with just a little advance work.

As with many things throughout this book, what follows in this section is not an all-inclusive list; it's simply perspectives from our family's experience, infused with ideas that came to mind as I was writing. Research and feedback prompted additional content, including the anecdotes from individuals whom I've quoted in the book. As you read, you may think of even more ideas. Jot them down in the margins to reference again later.

The early days of a travel sports journey are all about getting to know the organization and going to those first tournaments with the team. And so that's where we'll start too. From there, we'll journey through the season and off-season, then wrap things up with some thoughts on caring for people (including yourself) along the way. May this truly be a springboard to meet the unique needs of your family in the travel sports journey.

Chapter 1
Prepping for the Huddle

Prepping for a huddle with your player is all about foundation building. It's about having conversations with key people to learn expectations, gain understanding, and gather information. And one of the early conversations is close to home—being on the same page as parents before talking with your son or daughter.

Being on the Same Page

Some of the things you might tackle as parents before talking with your player include confirming existing family guidelines relative to the specific team and travel situation, discussing any changes in those guidelines, and considering what may be negotiable (or a combination of all three). Then ask yourself some questions to be prepared for the fluidity that comes with having a huddle. As parents, what initial decisions are firm? Which decisions have room for adjustment and change? What additional information do you need?

DID YOU KNOW?

Before 1893, pitchers threw pitches from a pitcher's box rather than a pitching rubber.[1]

The conversation doesn't have to be long—just a place to start so you can be on the same page as parents. New information or changes in information may impact the decisions you make with your player. And your son or daughter will probably have some ideas, opinions, and suggestions of their own anyway. Approaching the huddle as a discovery process that involves everyone allows layers of input and mutually beneficial decisions.

What about the Coaches?

Even in this early stage, coaches are essential in preparing for a huddle with your player. Getting to know a coach's preferences and style gives perspective and context to the information you are gathering about the team and organization. While this is always an ongoing process throughout your time with the team and organization, early observations and knowledge are a helpful part of the huddle framework.

DID YOU KNOW?

"The London Times was the first newspaper to publish daily weather forecasts in 1860."[2]

Look at the organization's website, attend informational meetings, and observe and actively listen whenever you are around team events with the coaches. Use discernment, especially in getting to know new coaches and organizations, but don't be afraid to ask questions about logistics or expectations to make sure you have the most current and up-to-date information.

Depending on your player's age and how comfortable you feel about the coaches having your son or daughter's contact information, consider involving your player in this advance work. Give your son or daughter ownership in the huddle prepping process with encouragement to ask coaches for information and then discuss it with you. Connecting with coaches early on also helps your athlete begin to show initiative and build positive relationships with the coaches.

Here are some questions to explore:

➤ Who will be responsible for players' time off the field in the event of bad weather or canceled games?

➤ What kinds of preferences and priorities are important to the coaches for the players' planned (or unexpected) downtimes?

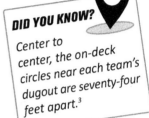

DID YOU KNOW?

Center to center, the on-deck circles near each team's dugout are seventy-four feet apart.[3]

➤ What are the coach's opinions and perspectives on workouts, drills, and practices outside of games during a tournament? Does it matter who initiates the training (coaches or players) and whether it is a solo or group endeavor?

➤ What are the coach's expectations of players at the hotel?

➤ Does the coach want the players to use the hotel's exercise room, pool, or jacuzzi before games or during other downtimes?

➤ How will communication be handled as schedules change during tournaments?

➤ How will team members communicate with each other during tournaments?

➤ If the team or organization already has an online group set up for general information, are new groups set up for specific trips and tournaments?

A Backdrop of Grace

Whoever is asking questions and gathering information (whether it's you, your child, or both) in preparation for a huddle, be respectful in approaching a coach—wherever you are on the journey with that particular coach and team. As a parent, you have a unique position and relationship with your child. Be confident in that. Trust your instincts. And in all of that, treat the coaches as you would want to be treated. A coach who feels interrogated, challenged, or argued with will naturally bristle like a porcupine. Be curious, pleasant, and respectful—not demanding.

While you may not always get the response you are hoping for, communication is a two-way street impacted by "traffic" or "noise" in either lane. You never know what kind of extenuating circumstances might be happening behind the scenes in a coach's life. You also may not realize how you are coming across to someone or how your life situations are sneaking in the back door to impact the conversation. At times during our journey, communication with coaches was part of my learning curve because I was tired, preoccupied, on deadline, or worried about personal situations as I talked with a coach. Even with a learning curve, though, it was still worth the effort to try.

DID YOU KNOW?

You might be surprised to learn that the baseball term "on deck" is a nautical reference. To be "on deck" meant to be above board in the open, main area of the ship. The baseball term "in the hole" also finds its origins in the nautical world, with the phrase referring to being below the ship's deck.[4]

Just as you pay attention to *how* you broach a conversation with a coach, pay attention to *when*. The middle of practice, between innings, or right before you leave for a tournament probably isn't the best time. Give that backdrop of grace by planning necessary conversations for your preparations as far out as possible. If you are feeling a strong nudge to talk right away, pause for a moment. Sometimes the nudge is for now; other times, the nudge is for praying, trusting, and being ready for the right opening.

Be discerning before and after practices and games too. If coaches are trying to set up, strategize, recap with each other, talk to players, or get to other appointments themselves, another time may be better. Contacting a coach later to schedule an appointment to talk (with or without your player) may be the best solution at times, suggests Trish, whose kids enjoyed various sports, including baseball (and travelball), karate, cheerleading, trampoline, and dance. If the coach has initiated a conversation, follow the coach's cues for the type and extent of your conversation. Don't take it as automatic permission to say everything on your mind and delve deeply into topics that may be best left for another conversation or time.

Being as prepared as possible for the huddle isn't about having absolute control or knowing everything at that moment. Once the season starts, there are always factors beyond our control (and sometimes even for the coaches). Hold your preparations and plans loosely since logistics or details may unexpectedly change.

For one early-in-the-season tournament with a new team, my son's primary coach (who was attending the tournament as one of the team's coaches) got sick the day before the team left and could not attend. When coaches who were unfamiliar with some of the players stepped in to lead the team that weekend, our son had the opportunity to adjust to new leadership styles, game plans, and tournament approaches. As he kept a good attitude, played his best amidst the changed circumstances, and initiated conversations with the coaches well, the experience stayed positive. He was able to make substantial contributions to the team in areas that interested him. He was also able to build coach relationships that set the tone for that tournament and future games and tournaments.

On Deck and Ready to Go

Whether you are prepping for your first huddle with your player or a later one because of new information or changing circumstances, keep the tournament location, tournament length, and age of your player in mind to help focus your questions and information gathering. If you are someone who likes to make lists and, even better, loves checking items *off* the list when they're done, the following page gives you space to do exactly that. Use what is there as a springboard and add to it or make a different checklist for this chapter. The next chapter, which is all about having the huddle, includes discussion topics and corresponding question prompts.

BUILDING YOUR CHECKLIST
GATHERING THE INFO

PARENTAL FOUNDATIONAL DECISIONS

DIVISION OF LABOR FOR HUDDLE PREPPING

COACH'S STYLE AND PREFERRED METHODS OF COMMUNICATION

TEAM REQUIREMENTS

ORGANIZATION, TEAM, AND COACH EXPECTATIONS

Chapter 2
Having the Huddle

The tournament location, tournament length, and your player's age will often impact any huddles you have with your player. In the story I shared earlier of me sprinting across the hotel lobby as cars pulled away outside, our player was a freshman in high school and on his first travel team. We were still getting to know families and didn't have everyone's contact information yet. As my husband and I talked with our son in some quiet moments after he returned from the outing, it was important for us to try to balance factors like trust, responsibility, and mutual courtesy during the conversation—rather than tight control. Since we were already in the middle of that tournament's trip, we also wanted to keep the excitement going in this new adventure and set everyone up for success over the rest of the weekend. Check-in policies were one area we discussed; other huddle topics could be the hotel, community, fields, and sports complexes.

Check-in Policies

When it came to family check-in policies, we clarified aspects of the "who, what, when, where, and how" surrounding activities and timing. For example, what kinds of activities off the field and in the downtime did our son need specific permission from us to do? Did he have to connect with us in person, or could he check in via a text, call, or note? And since both his dad and I were at this particular tournament, who did he need to check in with—both of us or just one of us? Related to "what" and the "who" was the "when." How often did we want our son to check in? For example, should it be at specific times during the day, after games, when an activity or outing came up to do, when something on the schedule changed, or a combination?

DID YOU KNOW?

William Gray, credited with the design of an improved chest protector for catchers, also invented the phone booth.[1]

The Hotel and Community

The "who, what, where, and when" of spaces, people, and outings may be the starting point for any hotel and community huddle discussion. For example, when is it time to exit another player's room so everyone can get some sleep? What and where is free roam space in the hotel, and is any area off-limits (from your perspective as well as the hotel's rules and guidelines)? What activities are OK at the hotel and in the community?

Besides being a team and family meeting place, a hotel may also serve as a community launchpad. When it is, talking through the community and the logistics of your son or daughter going off-site from the hotel may be important details to include in your huddle. Discussing decisions about opportunities beforehand can make deciding on those opportunities less stressful when they do come. Reviewing basic safety principles ahead of time never hurts either. And weaving in conversation about discernment and judgment in any activity or decision may be a timely contribution to any huddle.

For instance, what kinds of community activities (miniature golf, a mall, or restaurants) are accessible and OK for your athlete to do? Can your player go off-site alone or with other players? What about with players and other parents? For David, whose son and daughter played hockey, an essential part of them being able to ride with others was that the driver hadn't been drinking, so that was part of their family discussions.

Community and downtime logistic topics may also involve exploring questions like these with your player:

DID YOU KNOW?

Fenway's left-field foul pole is named the "Fisk Pole" after Carlton Fisk and his 1975 World Series Game Six home run for a Red Sox win in the 12th inning. In right field, "Pesky Pole" gets its name from shortstop Johnny Pesky whose homers often flew around the right-field foul pole on their way out of the ballpark.[2]

➤ Does the coach need to know when players are going off-site and how to get a hold of them?

➤ Do players, and especially your player, need to talk with parents or coaches while they plan activities or before they go off-site?

➤ How would everybody find out if the coach wants to have a practice?

At one tournament, our coach lost valuable impromptu practice time (even though he had everyone's contact information) because everyone was scattered. One of the fun things about travel sports is taking advantage of area sights. Consider the timing, though, in your planning to make sure activities fit with the bigger picture of the tournament schedule and team needs.

The Fields and Sport Complexes

Finally, let's talk about the ballpark—those diamonds of baseball—and the fields, courts, gyms, arenas, stadiums, and athletic complexes across the spectrum of travel sports. What options are available at the tournament if there are multiple games and time between games? And how would any check-in guidelines work there? Is there a group buddy system preference? What preferences, if any, does the coach have for the players' activities between games?

A Context for Everything

Take a few moments to reflect on your family's circumstances now. Sift through your thoughts and what you've read so far to find the nuggets of gold for you, your family, your specific travel situation, and what type of information you'll include in the huddle with your athlete. Write down key discussion areas for your upcoming huddle on an index card. Date the card and slide it into this book. In the book's margins, add any additional topics or questions that come to mind. Make a note to research those questions before the huddle with your player. As you do the research, keep the information accessible to refer to it quickly and easily as needed.

As you huddle, be judicious in sharing your key thoughts. An avalanche of details that smothers everyone and everything or creates panic, fear, doubt, or worry isn't helpful to anyone. Give your athlete, who likely also has ideas, time and space for responses and input. When it comes to conversations, remember that some

DID YOU KNOW?

While some accounts indicate that first baseman Charles C. Waite was the first player to wear a baseball glove on the field, A. G. Spalding is generally known for popularizing the glove and removing the stigma of wearing it. Spalding and his brothers then started their company, A. G. Spalding & Brothers, to sell gloves and sporting goods.[3]

meander while others focus on moving briskly to the end. For me, my energy level can also impact my interest in and pace of talking at times.

If your child is older and travels with the team under the supervision of coaches, other family members, or other parents, communication with those individuals is also a vital part of the conversation. Every situation cannot be anticipated and planned, but making an effort to have open and clear communication lays the groundwork to answer some situations' needs so they don't become an emergency or crisis.

Prepping for and having a huddle with your player. Thinking through and clarifying logistics. Getting to know the organization and coaches. The journey has already begun! Build your huddle logistics checklist on the next page. Then in the journaling journey-maker space that follows, take a moment to write, sketch, or draw a couple of your huddle high-fives before diving into the packing. Excitement and anticipation are around the corner. Soon there's some packing to do.

BUILDING YOUR CHECKLIST
A HUDDLE'S 5 Ws AND AN H

WHO: PARENT(S), PLAYER, ANY OTHER FAMILY MEMBERS

WHAT: TOPICS TO COVER

WHEN AND WHERE: DATE, TIME, LOCATION

WHY: PROACTIVE, REACTIVE

HOW: IN-PERSON OR USING TECHNOLOGY

Becoming a Journey-Maker:
Your Huddle High-Fives

Becoming a Journey-Maker:
Your Huddle High-Fives

Becoming a Journey-Maker:
Your Huddle High-Fives

PART II

Packing the Backpacks, Bags, and Boxes

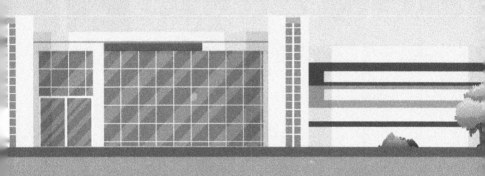

W hether clutched in hand, piled in a van, or tossed in an airplane cargo deck, they're the luggage of sports—backpacks, bags, and boxes. Our family had been packing for years to participate in single games, double-headers, and tournaments before we started with our first travel team. And with most of those pre-travelball games local or within a short distance from our home, it was easy to run back to the house or to a familiar store to pick up supplies.

Like a cross-country trip or overseas vacation, though, we quickly found that away games and multi-day tournaments requiring hours of driving or a hotel as a home base needed different strategies and expertise. While players don't want to forget anything they need in order to play, we didn't want to have to carry, push, pull, or drag anything that felt like a load of lard on the hips or a wheelbarrow weighted with twenty tons of bricks. So how can parents be prepared for the planned and unplanned, the expected and unexpected, the scripted and unscripted?

Pack the basics, put in some specialty focuses, add the layers, prepare for contingencies, and remember the icebox.

Chapter 3
Starting with Some Staples

I t all starts with mitts, shoes, bats, and a helmet—classic player staples stuffed into the baseball bat bag. Left-handed mitts will find their way into a left-handed player's bag, and position-specific gloves are also staples for many players. A lefty pitcher and first baseman, our son packed both a left-handed glove for pitching as well as a first baseman's glove. A wood bat and a practice bat joined the traditional aluminum bat in his bag. And molded plastic cleats for turf fields joined metal cleats and tennis shoes. With multiple fields and locations within a single tournament, all three pairs of shoes went to every tournament and every game. Whatever the sport, whatever the position(s), there are always classic staples and specialty tools to pack.

Ready for Anything

For outdoor sports like baseball, softball, soccer, and track, changes in weather and field conditions can call for a change in equipment at any time. Facility administrators, tournament organizers, and referee or umpire decisions can also impact a player's equipment needs. At one of our son's baseball games toward the end of a season, an unexpected on-the-field decision by leadership meant players needed to pull the aluminum bats out of their bags when wooden bats had been the standard all season.

When it comes to shoes, last-minute field changes, wrong information about the field's playing surface, or even field regulations may require a footwear flip. On a turf field for one of our baseball games, metal spikes and cleats were not allowed at all, while plastic and molded cleats could be used anywhere except the pitcher's mound. On the pitcher's mound, tennis shoes were required—at least on that day, on that field, in that game, with those umpires, and with those opposing team coaches. Having both staples and specialty equipment at my son's fingertips in his game bag made field adjustments quick and less stressful that day.

DID YOU KNOW?

The plastic coating at the end of a shoelace is "called an 'aglet,' and it comes from the French word for 'needle' (aguil-lette)."[1]

Regardless of the sport, sometimes packing hiccups happen when families leave things behind. And when players pack their bags, forgetting anything can lead to excellent problem-solving, creativity, and character-building opportunities. David remembers his kids packing for out-of-state tournaments simultaneously one week and inadvertently switching their hockey pants. Since the household rule was that if they forgot anything, they would not be able to participate, his resourceful kids quickly arranged to borrow hockey pants from fellow players so they could compete.

Snack Staples

Sunflower seeds are a ballpark classic and start the snack chain for many baseball players. When our son spotted flavored sunflower seeds in the dugout and then in stores, he sometimes included those in his player bag. He also often added protein bars, beef jerky, and trail mix to the sunflower seeds.

Some snacks make the team, though, because of the stories behind them. The snack is fun, easy to eat, associated with having a good game, or an "inside team joke." Linda's son was on a team whose favorite "inside joke" snack turned into a dugout tradition: Twizzlers. And it all started with ice, or rather, the lack of ice. One day, when the team needed ice in the dugout, it was nowhere to be found. As a search got underway for an alternative supply of ice, one of the players offered everyone the Twizzlers he had brought to the game that day. Twizzlers were at every game after that.

> **DID YOU KNOW?**
>
> Sunflower seeds are packed with six grams of protein per ounce.[2] Geography influences the number of flowers, or heads, on a sunflower. "The cultivated sunflower only has one flower or head. But the wild cousins found growing in ditches and other areas throughout much of North America have multiple flowers and heads."[3]

Water bottles tucked into bags; coolers rolled into sports complexes, stadiums, and arenas; and thermoses and jugs carried into dugouts are standard containers for players in any sport. At one of our baseball games, I saw a player carrying a store-bought gallon of water to the dugout like I carry a gallon of milk from the grocery store into my house. Electrolyte-enhanced drinks frequently get added to the mix of beverages too.

While we were never far away from stores in our travels, planning kept expenditures down and energy up. For our family, we packed individual water bottles (sometimes refillable ones, sometimes plastic disposable ones), as well as portable snacks and lunches for longer days. Dried fruit, pretzels, crackers, granola bars, rice cakes, peanut butter, apples, oranges, and pears are just a few ideas. Bulkier snacks, larger quantities of treats, and extra food stayed in the car and in coolers that we could get to easily as needed. You'll find additional food and cooler ideas in chapter 6, "Remembering the Icebox."

Clothing Basics

The last thing we wanted to do on our journey was to spend time and money buying clothes we already had at home. As our miles on the road increased, having some basic clothing layers and options close at hand in boxes, bags, and backpacks to adapt to whatever situation we encountered became even more critical during our years of travel baseball. Games started early, late, and anytime between; the weather could vary throughout the day and night; activities could unexpectedly switch from outdoors to indoors in a minute; and meals could flip-flop between picnics, a fast-food drive-thru, or a restaurant dining room at a moment's notice. During one tournament weekend,

- Roll clothes instead of stacking clothes in the suitcase to cut down on wrinkles and to conserve space.
- Create suitcase "sections" to make it easier to find things and pull items out quickly.
- Have the first night's sleepwear (and maybe even the next morning's outfit) in the top layer, an inside corner, or an outside pocket of your suitcase for quick and easy access in case of exhaustion when arriving late at a hotel.
- Consider strategically placing exercise clothes for easy access if you will be working out soon after you arrive.
- Put liquids in plastic, sealable bags when you pack to protect clothes in the event of spillage.
- Store duplicates of items you routinely pack together so you can grab and go, rather than having to take individual items in and out of cupboards and dressers to pack every time you travel.
- Keep travel sizes of personal hygiene items filled up and ready to go as part of what is stored together (either purchased travel sizes or travel containers you've filled yourself).

as thunderstorms interrupted a warm, sunny day to delay the games, we put our food coolers back into the car and pulled out lightweight jackets and sweaters as we went for lunch in an air-conditioned sub shop with another player's parents.

Since our family lives in the Midwest, we had already spent many years layering up for cooler temperatures in early spring and late fall. We even had a spring opening day one year when a light dusting of snow had covered the field the day before. We were familiar with sweatshirts, jackets, hats, gloves, scarves, earmuffs, and winter coats—with lots of extras in the car as we started the season. We routinely carried multiple blankets in the car too.

Now we also had to think about the other end of the temperature scale with extreme heat and humidity. At a tournament in a southern state, I quickly found that, for me, heat, humidity, and sweat mixed with clothing could lead to chaffing and very raw skin. I changed my skincare routine and incorporated more breathable, light-weight layers of clothing. With each trip (and a little bit of trial and error), figuring out the right clothing basics for various tournament conditions became easier.

DID YOU KNOW?

Wilson A. Bentley photographed thousands of snow-flakes and donated 500 of those photographs to the Smithsonian in 1904. His book Snow Crystals (coau-thored with William J. Humphreys) was first published in 1931.[4]

Wallets and Pockets

For parents and fans, wallet and pocket staples in backpacks, bags, and boxes include phones, cameras, cash, and keys. Of course, car keys are essential, along with multiple keys to your hotel room. And if you usually pick up keys just for the adults, consider getting an extra key for your player. Cash isn't necessarily needed for concession stands anymore since many of them take other forms of payment. If you pack your food and can bring that food into the stands and sports complex, cash isn't necessarily needed then either.

However, cash may be the only option at venue gates when there is a game or tournament entrance fee. Sometimes you can find the cost of those entrance fees on tournament websites, but not always. So, save yourself some stress and plan ahead. Research entrance fees online (starting with the tournament you are attending) and talk to your fellow journey travelers. They may even have attended that particular tournament in the past and know exactly how much the entrance fee was the year they went. Then have some cash on hand to cover the amount you anticipate (plus a little more). After going on a frantic search a time or two for cash right as a game was starting, we learned to make sure that we double-checked our pockets and wallets before we left to go to the tournament. Extra cash also comes in handy for meals with other parents, team dinners, or player hangout time. At one tournament, game-time changes due to overnight rain meant that players had plenty of time to get in a game of miniature golf after a hitting workout at a local facility.

• When preparing for potential entrance fees, have smaller bill denominations to make up the total amount you are taking with you. The person at the entrance gate may not have change for larger bills.

Photography equipment is a must-have packing staple, too—whether it's the cell phone in your pocket or another style of camera. Many times, just being present, enjoying the game, and loving watching your son or daughter play makes the memories and brings the joy on the travel sports journey. Sometimes, though, you want to add those memories to the family photo album. In baseball, it could be a great throw, superb catch, phenomenal pitch, fantastic base run, timely stolen base, marvelous slide, or glorious home run. Across sports, player moments abound as teammates give high-fives; coaches meet with players; teams walk into opening ceremonies; sons and daughters hold trophies; players gather to talk, eat, hang out, and cheer one another on; and athletes sit quietly, focused and reflecting as they prepare to enter a game.

Other times, your photography and videography are all about the fun signs, interesting architecture, and beautiful scenery you discover along the way. Whether it is a game or travel day photo, the snapshots I have bring a smile to my face when I look at them. (I've included some of those pictures in galleries later in the book.) Besides, taking photographs of unique ballpark features, fun ballpark signs, interesting equipment angles, and colorful complex grounds gave me something to do as we waited before games, between games, and after games. And like having some extra cash on hand for tournament fees and impromptu activities, remember to bring the battery packs, chargers, cables, and cords you might need for your cell phone and camera equipment.

Lights and Flights

Now might also be the time to start planning for any driving, flying, and home front preparations. If you're driving, make sure your car headlights, rear lights, brake lights, and turn signals work. Check your car's glove compartment and trunk crevices for up-to-date maintenance, safety, and emergency supplies, like the car owner's manual, a tire gauge, insurance cards, jumper cables, flares, a working flashlight (with extra and new batteries), and a first aid kit. Insurance companies and other organizations like the American Automobile Association (AAA) often have travel tips on their website. And whether or not you are already an organized person, resources like

DID YOU KNOW?

Millions of luggage cases and travel/sports bags are sold in the UK and the U.S. every year.[56]

the tips in author Stacey Platt's book *What's a Disorganized Person to Do*[7] titled "A well-stocked glove compartment," "Your car's emergency kit," and "First aid essentials" can help you create a personal car staples collection or road trip checklist.

Shelley, whose daughter played club volleyball, says, "One thing that was important for me when we traveled was the preparations I had at home in order to leave: stop the newspaper, water plants, turn on key lights, arrange a day (or days) of vacation, make flight arrangements (early!), reserve parking at the airport, and take the dog to the kennel."

Even travel preparations on the sports journey can turn into an adventure. Shelley remembers when their dog got some extra riding time in the car on the way to the airport. "One time, we arrived at the airport so easily. I had calculated it would take longer, but we got there quickly. When I looked in the rearview mirror as I was opening the rear hatch door, I saw the dog still in the car. I had forgotten to drop the dog at the kennel!" With rebooked tickets in hand from the airline, Shelley and her daughter took their dog to the kennel and then made it back to the airport in time to board the new flight and get to the tournament.

Now that you've begun to pack by gathering the basics, adding position-specific gear, checking wallets and pockets, and incorporating home front preparations, there's more to look forward to. "The travelball experience is the whole experience," says Brian Holman, who occasionally traveled to tournaments as a player himself growing up and also experienced a season of travelball as a parent and coach when one of his kids played baseball. "It's everything. It's the time spent in the stands. It's the time spent on the road. It's the time spent at the hotels and the pools and the restaurants. It's all part of the experience." A right-handed pitcher, after high school Brian played professionally first with the Montreal Expos organization (minors and majors) and then with the Seattle Mariners. Today, Brian speaks professionally, works with athletes of all ages all over the country, and coaches locally.

It's around that whole experience additional layers of packing, planning, and preparing come for exploring, learning, and having fun on the travel sports journey. So even as you fill suitcases and duffle bags with essentials, leave some space. The next chapter expands on this section's packing theme with layers of ideas for on and off the field. Factors like budgeting needs, who is traveling, whether the trip is doubling as vacation time, and family members' personality styles will influence what (and how many) ideas resonate. Adding layers is simply about getting the most out of the experience as you go, in ways that avoid stress and meet your family's needs, interests, and personalities. Build your staples checklist, and then head on over to the next chapter to explore the topic of adding layers.

BUILDING YOUR CHECKLIST

THE STAPLES

BACKPACKS, BAGS, AND BOXES

WATER AND SNACKS

CASH, CAMERA, KEYS, PHONE, AND CHARGER CABLES

HEAVY COATS OR LIGHTWEIGHT JACKETS

HOME AND CAR PREP

Chapter 4

Adding the Layers

L ayers of creativity and additional supplies build on the travel essentials you've already packed. They're layers for yourself, your player, the team, and your family. It's the time and energy spent enhancing the travel sports journey with brainstorming, ingenuity, and resourcefulness. It's the ways you find to fill the minutes before a game starts, the hour(s) between games, and tournament downtime. There are lots of ideas ahead, so regardless of whether you're adding one layer, lots of layers, or trying different layers from competition to competition, incorporate what makes sense for the pace that fits you and your family.

Between the Games

Whether it's a practice, game, or tournament, the wait could be long or short, during hot or cold temperatures, or with rain or sun. Whatever the delay, time occupiers are an important layer in the world of travel sports. It's also a layer that's easily forgotten in a rush to get out the door. So, take a few minutes to prioritize packing and planning for this valuable layer as you get ready to travel.

Just like at local tournaments, players often want to relax between games on the road by sitting and chatting, grabbing a snack, zoning out on their cell phones, watching another game, or wandering the sports complex. As backups for your player, slip things like decks of cards, travel games, books, yo-yos, and juggling balls into those backpacks, boxes, and bags as you're packing.

If siblings are coming along, include them in the planning and preparation. Put together a travel bag of time occupiers and fun things for them to do on the journey. Combine some of their favorite things with special items that only get packed for road trips or maybe even just for tournaments. If siblings have schoolwork that needs to get done, don't hesitate to pack some schoolbooks for them too. We've done homework in the car and at picnic tables by a field. And like the travel game suggestion earlier, games of all kinds are great for the family, too—whether it's for indoor play, outside on picnic tables and blankets, or in the grassy areas around park playgrounds, fields, and hotels. Some games in our closet that travel well on the road are UNO, Yahtzee, Mastermind, Spectrangle, Rack-O, Bananagrams, Rook, Phase 10, Qwirkle, and Dutch Blitz.

For yourself, take that novel you've wanted to read, a project you are working on, or a craft to finish. If you are on a work-related deadline, maybe toss that project in your bags too. You never know what ideas a change of scenery could bring. (Keep any project expectations realistic, though, so you still have space and time to enjoy the games, build relationships with other parents, and maybe even take some walks

DID YOU KNOW?

Beth Johnson (USA) holds the record for constructing the largest yo-yo. On September 15, 2012, she demonstrated a wooden yo-yo named Whoa-yo that she had spent three years constructing. It measured 11 feet, 10 inches in diameter and weighed 2.3 U.S. tons. The disc plunged 120 feet on a rope that was attached to a 75-ton crane before it rebounded.[1]

around the sports complex as you wait. The travel sports journey is about more than just games, scores, and logistics.) If you like to sketch or draw, grab a handful of supplies that travel well to create a visual journal of the tournament's places, people, and experiences.

Like the mobile art supplies just mentioned, fun writing tools are another interesting element to include in these layers you are adding. I've caught up with thank-you notes between games and written

DID YOU KNOW?
"'Schoolmaster' is an anagram of 'the classroom.'"[2]

letters during longer chunks of free time on the road. Whether you are writing on store-bought cards or adding a couple of lines to what you create with the art supplies you bring, the gift of time and penmanship through a handwritten note could be a treasure your friends and family cherish for years to come. I've kept many of the handwritten notes and recipe cards I've gotten over the years, and they bring a smile to my face when I come across them. Some of that handwriting is multi-generational from my mom or grandma. So, in a world of emails, texts, messages, and voicemails as daily go-to communication methods for many, consider occupying your wait times with notes to family and friends on unique cards and stationery. And remember to bring your address book and stamps so you can mail those creations right away.

These are just a few thoughts to get you started on planning and packing time occupiers for between games. You'll find more inspiration for everyone in Appendices A ("Packing the Sibling Activity Bag") and B ("71 Things to Do in an Hour") of this book. Check the lists out before you start driving, and of course, take this book with you to jog your memory as you go and add ideas.

In the Downtime

Longer stretches of time during tournament downtime open possibilities for adding even more creative and fun layers to enhance the travel sports experience. That downtime may come in the middle of a game day, at the end of a day, or during a "bye" or off day. The ideas and activities could revolve around team commitments, school or work responsibilities, hobbies and interests, or family and friends. Making the most of downtime often comes through a combination of planning and impromptu decisions—like the times when you decide to meet a parent in the hotel lobby on the spur of the moment for a quiet cup of coffee or sneak in a nap before you head out to do the next thing.

DID YOU KNOW?

The odds of a person always dreaming in color is 4 in 5.[3]

If you're traveling when school is in session, layer in study materials and homework by packing the books and scheduling study time. I mentioned earlier in the chapter that our car and picnic tables by the field were places we used to get sibling homework done. When it comes to your player, find out if coaches plan to organize any on-the-road study groups (whether your player travels with the team or the family) and take advantage of that option if needed. (One note, if your son or daughter is older, this question about study groups is more than likely a conversation for your player to have with the coaches.) If study groups aren't planned, talk with your son or daughter about working with the coaches or players to initiate one. And if that doesn't work, or no one else needs to study, strategize with your athlete about how to get studying done.

Facilitate opportunities for team members to engage with each other off the field by packing travel games, board games, decks of cards, a football or frisbee to throw around (in addition to the ever-present baseball for baseball players), compact and portable lawn games, hacky sack, and sport-related video games. Some of the more realistic video games enable you to set up teams for a virtual tournament. Make sure to bring along enough controllers so several people can play at the same time! Food is always a crowd-pleaser, and team dinners (with or without parents) are another way to build relationships and memories during downtime. Shelley remembers a special night at one of their volleyball tournaments. "One evening during a three-day tournament was a night where we had a team dinner and the girls dressed up," she says. "They loved that."

Spending time with family and friends in the area could also be a part of this downtime layer that adds to the travel sports experience. It could be an overnight stay, a short visit, or over a meal (with or without your player). When Shelley and her daughter traveled to our area for a tournament one year, we met up to watch the game and then visited for a bit. At one of our tournaments, we had a lovely lunch with a friend we hadn't seen for more than twenty years. At another tournament, we stayed with extended family we hadn't seen in several years and enjoyed getting reacquainted with them. Of course, invite those family and friends to the tournament too!

- As you reconnect with family and friends around tournaments, remember that camera you packed to capture momentous game moments, nostalgic scenes, and interesting landscapes? Do something that I wish I had done more of— take the camera out during those gatherings. Get group shots and individual shots. Take a few minutes to capture the joy, celebration, laughter, and maybe even the seriousness or quietness that comes up in those friend and family gatherings off the field. Then come out from behind the camera lens to immerse yourself in your surroundings once again.

- As you travel to various fields, wherever you are staying (hotel, campground, with friends or family), or whatever is next, keep the camera accessible. You never know when that perfect photo opportunity might come along as you drive down the road—or what photography or photojournalism hobby or career interests those on-the-road photo moments might spark!

Beyond the Game

Sometimes, surviving and thriving in the travel sports circuit is about what happens beyond the game—adding a layer of research and versatile activities to help you maximize time on the road, take advantage of local sights, and multi-task. Taking advantage of circumstances and opportunities as a trip unfolds is one way to add this layer. Other times, it's about the advance work and thinking you do as you start to pack.

So, research the tournament area ahead of time for ideas. Ask your family members what they would be interested in doing or seeing. Then put any notes, atlases, maps (paper or digital), and bookmarked online sites you've discovered into your backpacks, bags, and boxes. Include tourist attractions, educational ventures, and open spaces for fun ways to spend any free time, as well as parks and practice facilities. Be open to possibilities as you pack and are on the road. Mix and match as you go with expenses ranging from no cost to splurges in order to create memorable moments that you'll treasure for years to come.

"One activity we have been doing for many years that has really stuck with our family is disc golf," Jennifer says. "It all started several years ago when we were going to be traveling out of state to a tourist destination for a baseball tournament. With a large family, just covering food and lodging for the week left little else to cover any of the 'extras.' While researching some of the free attractions, I came across the idea of trying out a local disc golf course. We bought everyone a disc before we left (a bonus is that discs take up very little space, are durable, and inexpensive). We had a blast and ended up trying out more courses in the area that week. Since then, we always pack our discs when we travel for baseball or pleasure, and locating courses is one of the first things our kids look forward to doing. Most courses are free, it's great exercise, and it's an enjoyable family activity that all ages and skill levels can do together."

One year our family prioritized researching parks and beaches before going to an off-season, out-of-state tournament in our first year with a new travelball team. My husband and son then arrived a day early to get acclimated to the weather since it was a warmer and more humid climate than our Midwest fall months. They used the beach and a local park they had researched for pre-tournament preparation and training—swimming in the ocean, running on the beach, and throwing long toss at the park. The time my son spent with his dad in conditioning and acclimating to the climate before they met up with the team paid off for him in his tournament that weekend. The day after the tournament, he and his dad took a pontoon ride before flying back home.

Collecting travel brochures was a tradition I grew up with and continued during travel sports. We picked up brochures from visitor centers, hotel lobbies, and the places we visited. As we did, we discovered interesting places beyond the game that expanded and enhanced our family's travel sports experience. At a Tennessee tournament, my husband and I went to the Country Music Hall of Fame and Museum, learned about the Nashville origins of the Goo Goo Cluster candy at its downtown Nashville storefront, and went to the Grand Ole Opry. During a tournament in the Midwest one year, we checked out historic Wright Brothers' sites on the way to a game. A stop at the Cincinnati Art Museum on the way home from that same tournament featured a Tiffany glass exhibit and lunch in the museum's Terrace Cafe. A couple of hours and a few miles down the road, we experienced the unique taste of Skyline Chili for the first time at a Skyline restaurant.

DID YOU KNOW?

John Lloyd-Wright's Lincoln Logs were inspired by one of his father's designs, Frank Lloyd Wright's Tokyo Imperial Hotel—a building designed to weather earthquakes. Lincoln Logs were inducted into the National Toy Hall of Fame in 1999.[4][5][6]

Your athlete's age, how long you've been with a particular travel organization, and your family life season will influence what happens in the time beyond the game. As our ballplayer got older and was with a specific travel team longer, our free time and flexibility increased. The Nashville highlights and Ohio stops we made were excursions tailored toward our interests and specific life circumstances. At the time, our ballplayer was in high school, sometimes traveling and staying with the team, and the youngest of our three boys. Chapter 7, "15 Ways to Pass the Time on the Drive," includes ideas for fun on the road when the whole family travels together.

A couple of other ways we layered in ideas and activities for beyond the game as we packed and planned were related to our son's post-high school goals. Since he was interested in playing college baseball, our high schooler did the research and advance work to connect with coaches at colleges in the tournament area. We also added college stops to our itinerary as we traveled to and from summer tournaments. These stops weren't about official college visits or making appointments with people. They were just about walking campuses and seeing different approaches to layouts, buildings, and landscaping. Initially, the stops tended to be quick, but over time, the enthusiasm grew, and it seemed that adding this layer was helping our son get a sense of what he might like on a college campus.

In the Nooks and Crannies

By now, you, your player, and your family have packed a lot in those backpacks, bags, and boxes. There are still a few more layers of supplies and ideas to add. One of these layers is primarily for moms and dads, is easily tucked into the nooks and crannies, and doesn't take up much room. It's abstract and concrete. It's intangible and tangible. It's thought and action. It's hospitality. And it yields an abundance of dividends for players, coaches, families, spectators, and yes, even the umpires and other officials.

For now, include some wipes, towels, napkins, plastic grocery bags, and hospitable thoughts in your backpacks, bags, and boxes. Later in the book, I'll talk more about how those all fit together. Before we unpack hospitality, though, there are still some supplies to pack in those backpacks, bags, and boxes to prepare for contingencies. Take a look at the "Layering Up" checklist on your way over to contingency planning and fill in the details to personalize it.

BUILDING YOUR CHECKLIST
LAYERING UP

PROJECT(S) TO BRING

SIBLING BAG(S) TO PREPARE

GAMES AND BOOKS TO PACK

PEOPLE TO SEE AND PLACES TO GO

HOSPITALITY SUPPLIES TO TUCK IN NOOKS AND CRANNIES

Chapter 5

Preparing Contingencies

C hange can happen in a moment. All of a sudden, it's there—
the unplanned, unexpected, or unscripted. The weather may
become stormy, the balmy day may become chilly, the cooler morning
weather may be in the mid-eighties by the afternoon, the wait at the
field may be longer, or an emergency could happen. And that's when
those backpacks, bags, and boxes of additional supplies save the day.

Spend any time at a game, whether it is with a travel team or not,
and they are there. Solid, striped, and zany patterns. Handles, cords,
and drawstrings. Straw, plastic, and canvas. Left in the car or carried to
the field, the container styles and materials are endless. The purpose
for them all, though, is the same—having a great experience no matter
what the terrain looks or feels like because you've prepared (and
packed) contingencies.

Here are some ideas of reserves to have on hand as you travel:

> ➤ For those times when the waiting is starting all over again
> because bad weather has lampooned a game from starting,
> continuing, or ending—the time occupiers discussed in

chapter 4 about adding layers as well as even more ideas in appendices at the back of the book will come in handy

➤ For even cloudy days—sunscreen could be useful

➤ For cloudy weather that decides to turn sunny—take care of yourself with sunscreen, lip balm, a visor or hat, sunglasses, and maybe even an umbrella to give shade and block the sun's ultraviolet rays

➤ For when the field is at the edge of a forest or surrounded by mosquitoes—mosquito repellent spray will be your friend

➤ For when cold weather turns even colder—extra sweaters, sweatshirts, scarves, socks, and blankets are a must; along with an insulated, warm, heavy-duty coat and hand-warmers (build your supply throughout the year at resale shops, from clearance racks, and in off-season sales)

> **DID YOU KNOW?**
>
> In 1999, a woman named "Auntie" Betty Webster (USA) collected and wore novelty sunglasses while she worked in a restaurant in Kamuela, Hawaii. Her collection of 1,506 designs was verified on October 2, 2015. She's known as the "Hostess with the Mostess," and she color-coordinated her sunglasses with her clothes. She's always looking for new designs and even has some fans who add to her collection.[1]

➤ For when the rain comes, but the game goes on—you'll be glad you brought an umbrella, rain poncho, raincoat, or waterproof rain jacket

David says, "I used to wear a golf rain suit, which is waterproof pants and a waterproof jacket," and Trish recommends a cost-effective way to protect car seats: plastic bags.

➤ For when the dew hasn't evaporated or when the rain has left misty benches—paper towels or rags, tarps, and blankets with waterproof backing help you stay dry

- For wind that cools the sun in the fall and spring months—consider taking lightweight, layering clothes and jackets like long sweaters and windbreakers
- For cleats that suddenly fall apart or are left at home, and for those times when you absolutely, positively need to go to the store because it is the only solution left—a map of the area and your cell phone (along with a battery pack, cell phone charger, and cord in case the phone battery is dead at precisely the time you need to use it) will save the day
- For scraped knees, splinters, bumped shins, and other emergencies—ice packs; water; Band-Aids; tweezers; a first aid kit; personal medical supplies like prescriptions, inhalers, and insulin; and written medical information like doctors' names and medicine allergies

When it comes to a first-aid kit and emergency supplies, the basics like ice packs and Band-Aids are often carried to games by team moms and coaches, depending on your athlete's age. At some complexes, items like heat/cold packs and first-aid kits are kept in supply boxes close to the game location. Older players may be responsible for personal medical supplies, especially if they are traveling with the team; the "just in case" scenario may mean that you decide to have backup supplies with you, too, when you attend a tournament.

DID YOU KNOW?

Rainfall falls into three categories: convective, orographic, and cyclonic,[2] and physics impacts raindrops. "The laws of physics restrain raindrops from getting too large before they break up into smaller droplets. Thus, about 0.25 inches (0.635 centimeters) is the largest a drop can get and still have the surface tension of the water hold it together."[3]

Delays, bugs, weather, and emergencies—any of these situations could lead you to unpack the contingencies you've packed. Another reserve cache to consider preparing: food. I remember one time when the hotel breakfast option where the team was staying wasn't what they anticipated, and the coaches didn't expect it to change during the tournament.

DID YOU KNOW?
Wind direction measuring techniques and devices over the years have included the direction smoke blows, how balloons move, wind vanes, Doppler sodar (sound radar), and lidar (light radar).[4]

Some players and families adjusted their schedules that weekend to include restaurant stops for breakfast. Coaches did runs to the store for bagels, cream cheese, and fruit. Protein shake mixes and supplies could also be picked up on a store run. If a player's family is attending the tournament and has packed a slow cooker or instant pot, ingredients to make oatmeal or a breakfast casserole (a quick online search would give recipes for both) could be added to the shopping list.

And for that all-important extra food at the game and on the road, consider bringing an icebox (aka cooler with ice) in the car. You'll find ideas for packing it in the next chapter. First, though, check out this chapter's checklist idea, "Rain or Shine, Here We Come!" and add an idea or two of your own.

BUILDING YOUR CHECKLIST
RAIN OR SHINE, HERE WE COME!

FIRST-AID SUPPLIES

WEATHER CHECKS HERE AND THERE

BUG REPELLENT AND SUN PROTECTION STOCKPILE

RAIN AND COLD WEATHER GEAR

FOOD AND SNACKS

Chapter 6

Remembering the Icebox

Whether it's keeping chocolate protein bars cool so they don't melt on a hot summer day, keeping liquids cold for rehydrating during a game, or an on-the-go meal and snack buffet—there's something for everyone in the icebox. Those extra supplies can be a great help in providing for your player on a hot day after a long game, satisfying starving fans when the weather puts you in a holding pattern, or having some quick nutrition available when it is impossible to go anywhere and get anything before the next game starts.

Mixing and Matching

Coolers for players and fans at games aren't new. Like his teammates, our son carried water bottles, jugs, and coolers into the dugout. Like other families, we brought coolers into the stands and onto the side-lines. When we started travelball, the time we spent on the road, at

DID YOU KNOW?
Koji Nakao of Japan set a record for the heaviest strawberry at 8.82 ounces.[1]

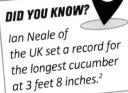

games, and in the heat of the day changed our packing. And it was a learning curve for us to plan for this kind of schedule.

One of the switches we made was to mix the sizes of drinks in our son's dugout cooler. Sometimes, several smaller bottles were more effective than larger drink containers that cooled down quickly and got too hot too fast.

Having a cooler in the car loaded with just the right kind and amount of extra food supplies became an important tool for saving money and nutritional balance. While we were never far from stores or additional resources, a store run didn't always fit neatly or well between games or into the logistics of early and late games.

Filling Up the Cooler

Here are some ideas of what to pack in coolers:

➤ water
➤ electrolyte-enhanced drinks, including electrolyte-enhanced water (one coach asked the boys to get Pedialyte on a particularly hot day)*
➤ finger-food snacks (cheese cubes, string cheese, pickles, sugar snap peas)
➤ finger-food fruits (grapes, apples, peaches, plums, nectarines, bananas, etc.)*
➤ make-ahead ideas (hardboiled eggs, celery stalks filled with peanut butter, cold fried chicken, sandwiches, salads, cut-up watermelon)
➤ ice pops (the ones that you freeze and then squeeze up the plastic—just make sure you have something with you to cut off the end of the plastic sleeve)*

* If packing high sugar or acidic drinks or foods, make sure to put a plan in place and be proactive in maintaining good dental hygiene to avoid annoyed dentists, nasty cavities, and high dental bills.

DID YOU KNOW?
Chris Kent of the USA set a record for the heaviest watermelon at 350 pounds 8 ounces.[3]

You'll find more great food ideas in two postings on Angela Weight's website (travelballparents.com), titled "Smart and Tasty Snack Ideas for the Ball Field,"[4] and "Ballpark Meals to Fill Them Up, Not Slow Them Down."[5] Contributors from across the country sent in their ideas, with many submissions containing purchasing suggestions, recipes, or pictures.

And for the ice? Purchase, help yourself, get creative, or all of the above. Convenience stores, grocery stores, and superstores are standard purchasing options. Sometimes hotels allow you to help yourself to their ice machines to fill up coolers; however, they also may have policies and signs posted asking you *not* to fill up your coolers with ice. And if all the stores are closed, you may need to get creative with making ice packs. Whether you make ice ahead of time or end up having access to a freezer on the road, see the ice tip at the end of the chapter for ways to make cooler ice packs.

Pulling Out a Classic

When a hotel or camper is home base, consider packing a slow cooker. A mom on one of our teams was a slow cooker wiz. One day, she brought hot dogs to the field that she had prepared in the slow cooker so everyone could eat between games. Another time, she used the slow cooker for chicken sandwiches. Her generosity was a blessing

DID YOU KNOW?
Hot dogs were among the first foods eaten during the Apollo 11 Moon mission. Heinz sells 11 billion single-serve packets of ketchup each year.[6]

and a treat—especially for those of us who generally wouldn't have something like a slow cooker on our radar.

An Instant Pot is another appliance that can be portable and function as a slow cooker. Get creative, try new recipes, and explore possibilities. Make your own icebox checklist on the following page, where you'll find five questions to ask yourself as you pack. You may want to add specific cooler items to the list or make another kind of checklist inspired by this chapter.

Even as you are brainstorming a good checklist and focusing on the finishing touches of filling up the backpacks, bags, and boxes, begin reflecting on your packing peaks (those highlights and successes that happen as you pack). Take a break to journal those packing peaks in the journey-maker space at the end of this section. Savor the moment and leave room for more peaks. Then let yourself dream. Give yourself the gift of time to start thinking about planning for fun and faith-building, so the journey of a travel team experience doesn't get consumed by busy schedules, tough game spots, and what feels like plain old work as an additional full-time, exhausting job. It's time to put some circuit breakers in place—no matter what path is ahead of you!

- Get creative with ice! You can buy several different types of ice packs at the store, and we have some of those that we often use. You can also create your own. Double layer sturdy plastic gallon bags, pour water in and freeze them. Then use the bagged ice block as an ice pack. While some water may seep out as the block defrosts, it should take a while since it is an ice block rather than chips or cubes. We also let our store-bought disposable water bottles do double-duty. Freeze the bottles, and they become the ice pack. Once the ice in the bottles starts to melt, you have cold drinking water.

BUILDING YOUR CHECKLIST
PACKING THE COOLER

WHAT FOOD DOES OUR FAMILY LIKE TO EAT?

WHAT FOOD WOULD BE FUN TO TRY?

ARE THOSE FOOD CHOICES NUTRITIOUS: DO THEY GIVE NATURAL ENERGY AND TRAVEL WELL?

WHAT CAN I FIX AHEAD OF TIME WITHOUT IT BEING STRESSFUL?

DID I REMEMBER THE ICE?

Becoming a Journey-Maker:
Your Packing Peaks

Becoming a Journey-Maker:
Your Packing Peaks

Becoming a Journey-Maker:
Your Packing Peaks

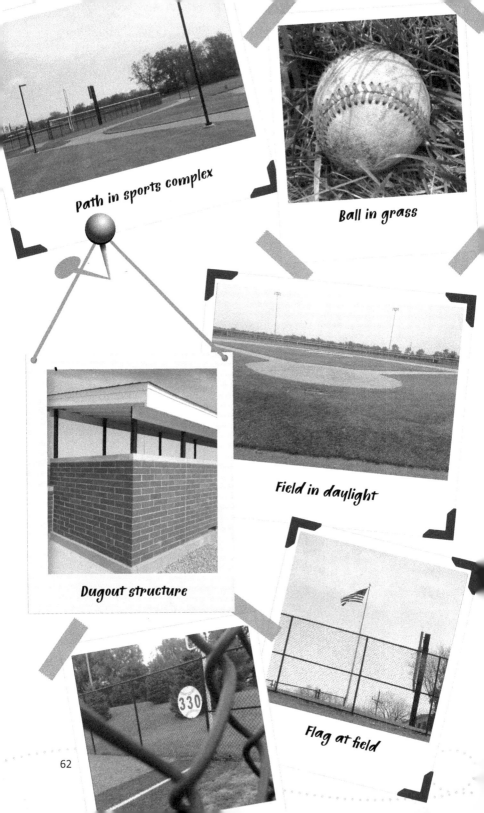

Path in sports complex

Ball in grass

Field in daylight

Dugout structure

Flag at field

Bats in the dugout

Fan stands

Field sign

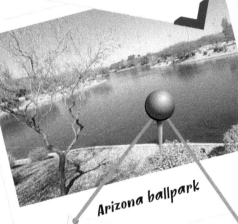

Arizona ballpark

Umbrella in stands

On-deck circle and helmet

63

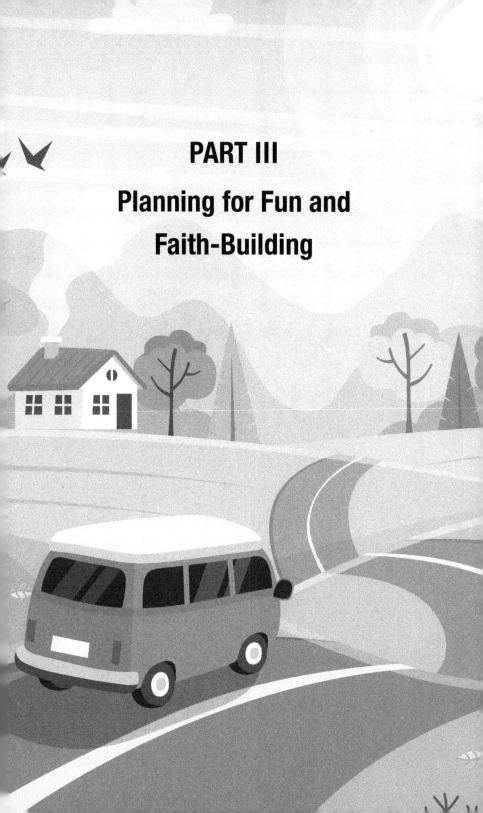

PART III
Planning for Fun and Faith-Building

The travel sports journey has lush, beautiful terrain rich with people, experiences, and games. Sometimes, the path isn't easy, though. Ups and downs. Twists and turns. Rough patches that make your feet stumble. All of it can impact the experience you have in the travel sports world. So how can you keep the experience fun amidst challenging terrain? How do you make memories along the way? How do you stay grounded in your faith and faith community if you have always attended church on the weekends, and it feels like there are always games scheduled Sunday morning? There are some solutions that make all those things possible—starting with turning the page to read the next chapter about ways to have fun on the drive.

Chapter 7

15 Ways to Pass
the Time on the Drive

C ity streets, rolling hills, crowded interstates, open highways—
being on a travel team means seeing a lot of landscapes over the
years. Our journey took us through small towns and downtowns, on
bridges and in tunnels, along railroad tracks and rivers, by farms and
skyscrapers, and past mountains and fields. Passing the time on a long
drive can be a challenge—or it can be an invitation to creativity. Check
out the list below to find a mix of solo and group activity ideas. You may
even recognize some of them from years past when you took family
road trips as a kid.

1. Count the number of different state license plates on
   passing cars
2. Play car bingo
3. Watch a movie or documentary
4. Listen to music
5. Tune in to talk radio
6. Rediscover classic radio programs

DID YOU KNOW?

"Mozart wrote the music for 'Twinkle, Twinkle, Little Star.'"[1]

7. Quiz each other on math facts, famous movie lines, sports trivia: the possibilities are endless
8. Read a book or listen to an audiobook
9. Take turns being the navigator using compasses, atlases, and printed maps
10. Write new songs
11. Have a sing-along
12. Talk to each other
13. Entertain a captive audience by reading aloud classics with jazzy vocal variety
14. Sleep
15. Make fun "pit stops" along the way

DID YOU KNOW?

The diamond on Arkansas' license plates gives homage to the state gem of Arkansas, a gem that the public can mine for at Murfreesboro's Crater of Diamonds State Park.[2] Giving a nod to inventors and aviation, one of the North Carolina plate designs has an image of the Wright Flyer on it. On Ohio license plates, a text background design includes the words "light and flight," "inventors," and "birthplace of aviation."

Books, games, music, and movies are easy to pack and unpack, and they are great for passing the time on the drive. "Pit stops" can also be a fun way to help "divide and conquer" the many miles of road trips, especially if you are taking the whole family and not everyone plays the sport or is playing in that tournament. Some stops may be planned ones.

"We'd go to water parks or stop at state parks and look [to see] if there was something fun there," Brian says. "You stay at hotels, and there's a cost, so you try to do other stuff. We might go see a Civil War battlefield museum. We'd make it about the family experience, and baseball was just part of that." Other times, the stop may be more spontaneous. "I was the dad that said, 'Hey, let's stop and see the World's Largest Ball of Yarn' or something goofy like that," Brian says. "We'd make it a fun time where it wasn't just getting in the car driving, sitting in the stands dying [from the heat], playing, and then turning around and leaving. We just tried to make it fun and enjoyable."

One spur-of-the-moment "pit stop" for our family one season was in Metropolis, Illinois, where we saw all things Superman. The city's town square is home to a colorful fiberglass fifteen-foot-high statue of Superman, a bronze statue of Lois Lane, a Superman-themed classic phone booth, and a storefront museum housing an overflowing collection of Superman memorabilia.

If you find yourself on Route 66 as you travel, have fun learning more about this interesting highway and keep an eye out for cool stops along the way. Route 66 is known by three other names: "Main Street of America," "Mother Road," and Will Rogers Highway. This historic highway winds across the country between Chicago and Los Angeles and is said to be more than 2,000 miles long with lots of iconic spots along the way.[3] If someone in your family has an interest in car racing, then speedway tracks across the country could be fun "pit stops." Some, like the Indianapolis Speedway track, may host a museum on the grounds and offer track tours. One interesting note about the Indianapolis Speedway revolves around bricks, pavement, and the start-finish line. Before pavement covered the Indianapolis Speedway track, a brick roadway was center stage. More than three million paving bricks replaced the track's first surface of crushed rock and tar. Reminiscent of that brick roadway is a remaining three-foot line of original brick at the track's start-finish line.[5][6]

DID YOU KNOW?

The first Rand McNally annual road atlas was published in 1924 under the name Auto Chum. Truck, rail-road, mountain, ocean, and lighthouse designs adorn its 2021 road atlas covers.[4]

You may not want to try to lead a sing-along, entertain everyone with a robust read-aloud story, or be able to make a "pit stop" when traveling by plane. However, many of the ideas listed in this chapter apply to plane, train, and bus rides too. Talking or having a family discussion—whether it's casual chit-chat or a deeply philosophical, theological, political, or emotional conversation—may be a harder place to jumpstart fun. However, it's not impossible. Conversation skills are teachable and learnable, and they're the subject of the next chapter. Before you get to chatting, though, make a "pit stop" to build your driving checklist. That itself may even jumpstart some conversation.

- If trivia is one way you want to pass the time on the drive, purchase trivia card sets or use index cards to make your own. Create a custom trivia card set around travel sports; specific aspects of a game or sport; individual or family hobbies; music, books, movies, or plays; career ideas; history; food; cities and towns; topics for developing subject matter expertise; or any other areas that would be fun for your family. If you don't have time to get, pack, or create a trivia set (or don't want to), lots of resources are available online by searching for trivia quizzes and lists.

BUILDING YOUR CHECKLIST
ALL ABOUT THE DRIVE

MAPS

PILLOWS

CAR TRAVEL GAMES AND ACTIVITIES

CLASSIC STANDBYS AND NEW DISCOVERIES

A FULL GAS TANK AND CAR EMERGENCY KIT

Chapter 8
The Art of Family Discussion

All those miles in the car mean lots of conversation opportunities. But it's not always easy to do when you don't know where to start; when you've run out of ideas after having already spent so many hours together; or when conversation doesn't come easily because of a person's skillsets, previous experiences, or personality traits. The art of conversation and family discussion can be challenging for any one or more of these reasons.

A Place to Start

When the week has been busy, or the day before filled with family members going opposite directions, sometimes the place to start is to just catch up. Ask general questions about how the week or day has gone. Ask specific questions about classes, homework assignments, lunchtime, and activities. Try to ask a mix of yes/no and open-ended style questions to facilitate responses and discussion.

Be sensitive to the kinds of questions you ask, though, if you have a group of kids in your car. What may be very comfortable for someone to share one-on-one may not be as safe in a group setting—even if

DID YOU KNOW?

A system and a code, the Braille cells for alphabet letters have six dot positions. A single cell of six dot positions can also be used for numbers, punctuation, or even words.[1]

it is just your child and their siblings. Tone is also often key even more than content here—especially as kids reach their teens.

Also, adjust your conversational focus to the timing and context of the car ride. Longer trips offer more time to delve into a subject or to cover a myriad of topics. And short trips may not always be the time for reminders about a "to-do" list. While it may seem effective and efficient to maximize those few moments when life is busy, it may not be the best way to build a relationship with your son or daughter.

Silvia often took her teenage son to the train station for travel to team practices and offers a good mom reminder. "It's important not to take that time to correct them or discipline them or remind them of all the chores they will have to do when they get home," Silvia says. "It's tempting because there seems to be such short times when we are with them, but if we want them to see our company as a good experience, we have to foster that."

Other times, the starting point comes from knowing your kids. It is an intentional effort to focus on them more than on what you want to know or a specific piece of information you want to find out. Drenda's family didn't take a travel team journey, but they were in the car a lot as they lived life together. "I'd ask the kids questions about things they liked or their thoughts, and then they're off," Drenda says. Games, movies, plays, or videos they've seen are also topics of interest for her family.

Absorbing the Moments

Once an activity or question has launched a lively discussion in a packed car—absorb the moments of jubilance. Listen to the conversation swirling around you. Enjoy the developing social skills you are hearing and seeing. Smile with the fun that is happening. Appreciate the burgeoning comfort level among the group as they talk to each other. Notice topics and comments that could be springboards for later conversation: long ones, short ones; challenging ones, easy ones; fun ones, serious ones; intriguing ones, thought-provoking ones; and unusual ones, as well as unexpected ones.

Enjoy the quiet moments, too, when it is just you and your player in the car— when it's a one-on-one moment instead of a group free-for-all. As questions spark conversation, practice active listening skills. Acknowledge what is said with a head nod or an "um hmm." Rephrase what is said. Ask a follow-up or clarifying question that avoids leading tones or word choices. Use the moment, first and foremost, to learn and understand. If context or time allows, offer

DID YOU KNOW?

Some consider the full chemical name of titin to be the longest English word at almost 190,000 letters. The largest known protein in muscle cells, titin is thought to contribute to muscle movement.[2][3][4][5]

insight, perspective, and personal anecdotes that build rather than preach. Opinions are often best heard when asked for, but even then, be careful to keep a window open rather than closing a door.

When Reticence Rears Its Head

What do you do in situations when the conversation doesn't come as easily, though? It could happen for a variety of reasons—quietness, mono-syllabic answers, different conversational skills, different conversational needs, or sometimes an athlete is simply too tired after a hard game or two to talk.

Be patient as you:

➤ chat in smaller chunks,
➤ find an alternative conversation focus,
➤ change your expectations, and
➤ take a long view.

Guide the conversation in smaller chunks of time and material. Vary the topics and the intensity of those topics. Intersperse conversation with other activities (e.g., listening to music, watching a movie, gazing out the window, reading a book). Turning on some music or other background noise could provide just the relaxation everyone needs at the moment and set the stage for conversation later. Try out some of those ideas from the earlier "15 Ways to Pass the Time on the Drive" chapter and add your own.

Sometimes, finding an alternative conversational focus that takes the pressure off others to initiate intense or deep levels of communication is what is needed. Sharing a positive, funny, or encouraging story from your years growing up might be one way to change the conversation focus. A trip down memory lane with your son or daughter sharing fun stories of the past might be another way that works well with your family.

DID YOU KNOW?
"During photo-synthesis plants use carbon dioxide to produce oxygen."[6]

Maybe the alternative focus comes from letting others start the conversation. Use chat packs, question cubes, or topical idea books that would spark easy and quick answers. Use written material as a conversation starter. Have someone in the car (who is not driving) read an article, a book chapter, or a news story and then talk about it.

The world and its landscape might be another source of conversation inspiration. Living in the Chicago area, the highways around us are often congested. Construction with gray, ugly concrete dividers and walls can often be a season that overshadows nature's seasons. And skies are not always clear. At an Arizona tournament, the clearly

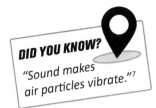

DID YOU KNOW?
"Sound makes air particles vibrate."[7]

visible mountains, landscaped freeways, and decorative dividers became conversation starters for me with my son.

Changing your expectations is also key in responding to a reticent talker. Being OK with silence may be just the right prescription when reluctance rears its head. The hesitation could be about skill and comfort level, but it could also be related to tiredness or personality traits that don't thrive on a lot of conversation. Not everyone needs to talk as much as everyone else. Thinking and pondering (or maybe even just resting) may be the need of the moment for your player. Remember that reminder from Silvia earlier in the chapter about fostering our company as a good experience? A welcoming presence allows for that resting or pondering and can be a bridge—and bridges can go a long way toward building relationships for those times of crucial conversation.

Another way to change your expectations could be in not always expecting long detailed answers or intense, in-depth conversations that go on for hours every time you get in the car. Instead, expect and embrace variety. Value brief answers that

DID YOU KNOW?
Did you know that a piece of confetti is called a "confetto"?[8]

are a little bit more than yes or no as much as you value a book-length response. Having valued two-, five-, fifteen-, or thirty-minute conversations along the way might be what is needed before having those important sixty-minute conversations.

Finally, take the long view, not just in responding to those who are slow to talk but in the whole concept of family conversation and

DID YOU KNOW?

A boat has a hull, bow, stern, port side, and starboard side.[9] [10]

discussion. It is all about learning and skill-building, and it is a process. It is an art that, with effort and intention, can develop more fully with each time in the car, each game traveled to, each tournament completed, and each season finished. Observation skills are an important part of all this. Areas to make a mental note of before, during, and after conversation lead off this chapter's checklist.

As you've planned fun ways to pass the time on the drive and engaged in conversation with others, memories are building. Your prepping and packing skills have been top-notch as you've incorporated tips from this book. And you're well on your way to traveling the travel team circuit without *constantly* blowing a circuit because of all the breakers and switches you are putting in place to prevent systems from being overloaded, shorting out, or losing power. Now it's time to do some more system construction as you plan for faith-building when games overlap with home church weekend services. Find out how in the next chapter.

BUILDING YOUR CHECKLIST
TO TALK OR NOT TO TALK?

MOOD

TIMING

BODY LANGUAGE

ENERGY LEVEL

PERSONALITY PREFERENCES

Chapter 9

When Games Overlap with Your Church's Weekend Services

Years ago, youth baseball and other sports weren't played on Sundays. Sunday was family day. A day of worship. Or just simply a day off, a day of rest. Today, Sunday practice and play are commonplace. For some families, the decision is a clear and definitive one that their son or daughter will not play sports on Sundays, and it's easy to reach an agreement with the team coaches and managers. Or it's easy to choose other interests that don't compete with your family's Sunday focus. For others, the situation is not quite so cut and dried.

This chapter dips into the family focus of a Sunday church tradition, something important to us over the years. If this material doesn't apply to you right now, turn the pages to the journaling journey-maker space at the end of the section and then onto the next chapter.

If you've historically had a Sunday church tradition, what do you do when there is a travel team conflict? How can an athlete be active and intentional about having faith, knowing God, and going to church? Thinking ahead is key for players and families, as well as planning to be at a weekend church service as much as possible, maintaining connections at church through volunteering or other opportunities, and getting creative.

Be willing to reevaluate the needs and seasons of your life because what worked before has changed. Be proactive about building your faith and relationship with God wherever you are. And be intentional about finding ways to gather with others to worship and fellowship that may look different than before. This was all a work in progress for our family throughout the travelball journey. Here are some ideas to get you started:

➤ Listen to the Bible on tape, CD, or via a phone app while traveling

➤ Take a hymnal or songbook to sing praise and worship songs together as you drive

➤ Ask someone to read from the Bible as you drive

➤ Listen to previous sermons on tape, CD, or digital media streams

➤ Stream your church service before or after the game

➤ Mark your calendars as you pick a service to attend (when your church has multiple service time options) even if it is not your "usual" time or means you would be sitting someplace other than your customary section, pew, or seat

➤ Be flexible when your church has services on Saturday and Sunday and go on whichever day you can

➤ Go to a mid-week service as a family

➤ Continue in your traditional volunteer areas at church or look for new ones that fit better with your new schedule

- Get to the field early to spend some time in Bible study, worship music, and prayer before the game
- Plan to do a Bible study, worship, and prayer time as a family before or after the game when it conflicts with your usual church service time
- Be proactive about doing your own personal Bible study
- Set aside family time to review the Bible verses everyone is memorizing and make that time a special family celebration
- Carry a memory verse pack everywhere you go, taking advantage of the minute moments of life to ponder and meditate on God's Word
- Gather other families from the team who might be church-goers and lead a service if you're away at a tournament
- Find a local church service to attend as a family or with other families on the team

DID YOU KNOW?

The "Feeding of the 5,000" miracle is recorded in all four gospels (Matthew, Mark, Luke, and John) of the Bible.[2]

Brian's family's time with God took several different forms as they traveled for sports and other activities throughout the year. A weekend boat or road trip might find them looking up and visiting a church when they couldn't attend their home church. "It was interesting to go to different churches and see different buildings and hear different messages," Brian says.

When tournament pool play or brackets resulted in early Sunday morning games, they'd spend time in the car talking about and studying

DID YOU KNOW?

Pitcher Orel Hershiser of the Los Angeles Dodges quietly sang "The Doxology" in Oakland Stadium's visitor's dugout between pitching outings during Game 5 of the October 1988 World Series match-up between the Dodgers and Oakland A's.[3]

the Bible. And other times, medical battles, like his daughter's leukemia, impacted the way the family chose to worship God together. "We went through a lot of hard things as a family," Brian says. "So, we spent a lot of time together, and church sometimes was held in a park or picnic area and [it was] something that we did as a family."

For some of you reading this, though, you grew up going to church on Sundays, and that was that—no discussion, no arguing, and no budging. Or perhaps you always planned on things being a certain way when you got older and had kids—and that included being in a church building at a worship service on Sundays. Yet life surprised you. Things didn't go as planned. Difficult decisions or circumstances arose. And now, finding the energy to be creative feels like an impossibility as practices, games, or being on the road increasingly overlap with weekend church services for your family or athlete.

For us, we never expected to have a family member passionate about playing a sport. Life also threw us many curve balls over the years. And as our son's passion for baseball grew, and that passion became part of who he was and his dreams and goals, Sunday play and travel sports were not one-dimensional issues. It became increasingly difficult to hold fast to an absolute no-sports-on-Sunday policy.

Since we had waited to enter the world of travel teams until our son's high school years, our family's life stage was integral to how we handled the whole travelball journey, as well as the processes and decisions relative to Sunday games and tournaments. (And this dilemma is not just a sports dilemma. We had the same kind of conversations and decisions to make relative to part-time jobs for our teenage sons.) We made a decision for our family; others make decisions for their families. Sometimes, those decisions match circumstance, opportunity, principle, technology, or community and culture. Sometimes, one thing takes precedence; other times, it is a blending of many things for the best decision at the time. And over time, that decision may change; that's OK. It may even change more than once; that's OK too.

If you're considering church commitments, Sunday principles, and life priorities relative to travel sports, the personal study titled "Sanctuary Required?" (Appendix C) later in the book is for you. Whether you're wondering, wrestling, or simply curious, there you'll find a place to begin to explore what the Bible says about church and Sundays. If you have time to do the study now, great, forge ahead on that and then come back here to pick up where you left off with what's ahead—a photo gallery and section about hospitality. If you are ready to move on, just keep reading.

Practicing hospitality can have an amazing impact on your own sports journey, as well as with your fellow travelers. As you get to the end of this section, though, first glance at this chapter's checklist on the next page and take advantage of the section's journey-maker space that follows to capture memories of your planning pinnacles and destination delights so far. Include a few words, a sketch, or a drawing—and leave space for more great memories. Then, browse the photos as you get ready to start unpacking hospitality in "A Smile and a Phone Booth."

BUILDING YOUR CHECKLIST
FAITH ON SUNDAYS—AND THE REST OF THE WEEK

CALENDAR CHECK
STANDARD OPTIONS
CREATIVE THINKING
PLANNING AHEAD
FLEXIBILITY AND FEASIBILITY

Becoming a Journey-Maker: Your Planning Pinnacles and Destination Delights

Becoming a Journey-Maker:
Your Planning Pinnacles and
Destination Delights

Becoming a Journey-Maker: Your Planning Pinnacles and Destination Delights

Photo Gallery 2

ON THE ROAD

Museum grounds at
an Indianpolis museum

Waterfall at an
Indianapolis museum

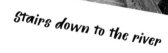

Stairs down to the river

Double rainbow

Lighthouse

PART IV
Unpacking Hospitality

You're in the car, van, bus, or plane. The prepping and packing are done, the drive or flight has started, and everyone has settled in for the journey. Soon the unpacking will start. One of the first things to unpack is one of the last things you packed—the mindset and trade tools that you put in the nooks and crannies of your backpacks, bags, and boxes. The idea of hospitality.

Hospitality is the touch of class that raises everything a notch. It builds reputations, friendships, and unity. It gives dignity to wins and losses. It's all about people and spaces. And it's the unique intertwining of people and spaces in sports and the travel journey that makes the topic of hospitality a part of this book.

Some of the discussion that follows will seem like common sense, yet common sense can quickly and easily evaporate in the excitement of a game. Traditional etiquette norms are continually being challenged with the proliferation of technology and hand-held devices at sporting events as much as anywhere. Other parts of the discussion may simply be gentle reminders of things you already do in other situations but haven't necessarily thought about them relative to this context.

Hospitality matters—even in the world of sports. The lead-off hitters for hospitality that matter and make an impact? A smile and a phone booth.

Chapter 10

A Smile and a Phone Booth

Stop, duck, and cover. It's the universal reaction to the "heads up" call as a foul ball rockets through the air toward the stands during a baseball game. Sometimes, duck and cover is exactly what you want to do as the fan sitting next to you suddenly bellows in your ear or a coach yells. Other times, you may feel the instinctive urge to raise your voice a thousand decibels in a full-throated yell to join the disappointed-fans-chorus that is responding to umpire calls and field plays with an

DID YOU KNOW?

Harvey Ball created the smiley face in 1963.[1]

off-pitch and out-of-tune sound that can be heard in the parking lot miles away.

There is another option, though: a smile. In the rush of getting ready to go, it's easy to forget to pack a smile. And in the drama of sports, it's easy to forget to unpack it. The good news is that whether or not you've forgotten to pack or unpack it—smiles are retrievable.

It's All in the Eyes

Retrieving a smile may be as easy as slipping down a wet slide or as challenging as searching for keys in a bag that feels like a bottomless pit. Putting on a smile may be as comfortable as a pair of old sweats or take as much effort as getting a rusty pump to work. And letting that smile genuinely travel from sparkling teeth to welcoming eyes may be as quick as ice melting on a hot day or as slow as the acclimation to cold ocean waters. Regardless of the effort it requires, or the time it takes, the benefits of a smile far outweigh the work. And smiles are not just for that loud fan, vocal coach, annoying umpire's call, or parents and players who are passing each other at the field.

Smiles reflected in the eyes matter off the field too. They are the hospitality extended among adults, as well as adults and players. It is a timely greeting when parents' paths cross in hotel hallways and at restaurants. It is the goodbye and "see you at the next game" shout-out when coaches and players are leaving the field. And it is part of the "hello" for those times when players cross paths with other team members' parents. (Even better, help your player get to know all the parents and their names to be able to give courteous greetings to all the parents when they do cross paths.)

A Virtual Phone Booth

Cell phones, on the other hand, are seldom forgotten or hard to find. And sometimes it would be nice if they came with booths like the days of old—pay phones in free-standing structures with walls and doors. As the booth design evolved, they were often made of clear glass or plastic. The person talking on the phone in the booth could still see what was happening outside, but there was a buffer zone between that conversation and the rest of the world.

Having to go into a booth to make calls was a win for both sides. The people who were participating in the event weren't distracted, the conversation among those not on the phone could still easily continue, and the person on the phone had privacy. If you decide to make or answer calls at the field, find a space that has the same buffer zone as an old-fashioned phone booth.

DID YOU KNOW?

There's history and intrigue in these area code numbers established in 1999 that are still in use today— Knoxville's "865" spells "VOL"[4] and Florida's Brevard County's "321" is all about the countdown.[5]

A smile and a phone booth, however, are just the beginning of unpacking hospitality. Use the checklist questions at the end of this chapter to spot check your hospitality quotient during the travel sports journey—or take an entirely different approach that would work best for you. Housekeeping and a proactive attitude in getting to know others on the team are two more key aspects of hospitality and also the subjects of the next two chapters.

BUILDING YOUR CHECKLIST
HOW DO I SOUND?

IS MY SMILE IN MY EYES, MOUTH, WORDS, AND GREETINGS?

AM I LOOKING FOR A QUIET, SAFE PLACE TO CHAT WHILE I ANSWER THE PHONE?

CAN I SIMULTANEOUSLY CHAT, WATCH THE GAME, AND KEEP AN EYE ON MY OTHER KIDS FROM THERE?

HOW CLOSE AM I TO OTHERS ON THE STANDS AND SIDELINES?

WOULD MY VOICE CARRY AND DISRUPT OTHERS CLOSE BY?

Chapter 11

Housekeeping on the Road

E ver notice how quickly open surfaces at home, like kitchen countertops and tables, can become covered with all things left behind as family and friends go about their day? Or how shared spaces become magnets for ever-expanding collections of one person's stuff, spreading onto someone else's shelf, desk, or bed? It happens in sports stands too. As you stake out a reasonable space for you and your family in the stands, beware of space encroachment and be considerate of others.

The Space

As a game ends, the little things can often get missed when packing chairs, blankets, and coolers (especially when you're in a hurry to get to another game, another team's fans are arriving to fill the stands, or you see bad weather approaching). At tournaments with many teams or when fields are not home fields, it's easy to assume others will do the work and not think about cleaning up your area in the stands.

DID YOU KNOW?

Boston's Fenway Park,[1] Illinois' Wrigley Field,[2] and Kansas' Newton Fischer Field[3] are on the National Register of Historic Places

- Start the pick-up process before the game ends. Plan ahead and don't wait until the last minute to start getting ready to go. Growing up, I lived on the East Coast and went into Washington, D.C., every year with my family for the Fourth of July concert[5] and fireworks. Mom packed a picnic dinner, and we'd leave in the afternoon to go downtown. Every year, Dad seemed to find the just-right parking spot that was easy to get in and out of, so we were home in a jiffy. And every year, Mom and Dad had us start picking up the blankets and picnic supplies as the firework finale was going off. We could still see the fireworks as we picked up, and every year we beat all the traffic in and out of D.C. Just like during the fireworks, you, too, can start picking up in the final inning of the game. Make a game out of it for your kids. And if it's a close game or nail-biting last inning you don't want to miss, have a quick-action backup plan in place to start as the teams take the field to congratulate each other.

Crumbs clumped like barnacles on ocean rock may not be the most comfortable seat for the person who comes along after you. Fine dustings of crumbs, while soft like a carpet of moss, also aren't exactly what the next person on the bench wants to sit in or find clinging to their clothes as they get in their car to go home. Candy or pop residue that is as sticky as sap isn't really what someone wants to scrub out of their pants either. And while signs can be useful in pointing the way to the field, empty wrappers and trash pointing the way to the stands aren't so welcoming. Choose a different path. Choose proactive hospitality. The more you do, the more it becomes second nature.

DID YOU KNOW?

"Of the more than 1,400 species of barnacles found in the world's waterways, the most common ones are called acorn barnacles."[4]

Remember those wipes, towels, napkins, and grocery bags you packed? Take some to the field because now is the time to unpack them: wipes for cleaning; napkins, paper towels, or a cloth towel for drying since no one wants to sit on a wet bench; and a grocery bag for trash.

The Check

As siblings go off to play, have them do a bench check first to pick up any crumbs or trash. Just as coaches tell players to clean out the dugout when they leave, pick up your stuff (and maybe even that single-use plastic water bottle someone finished and forgot) to toss in the trash can on the way out. If picking up someone else's empty can or plastic bottle bothers you, consider carrying a stash of disposable plastic gloves to quickly slip on and keep a travel size bottle of hand sanitizer in your supplies. Have a hospitality mindset and build the team's reputation.

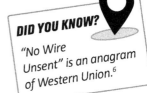

DID YOU KNOW?

"No Wire Unsent" is an anagram of Western Union.[6]

Include your own cues and prompts to help you remember to do this on the list that follows or create an entirely different kind of family checklist around this topic of hospitality through housekeeping on the road. Keep the fun. Add the care. Be the team you want to sit with and the team someone else wants to follow on the bleachers or stands.

tip

- Today when we check out of a hotel, the last person leaving the room does a visual check to make sure we didn't leave anything behind. In the same manner, do a visual scan of the stands before you go. Do you have everything you came with? Are you leaving only footprints? Is there anything else you, your family, or your player can help pick up? Is there anything else your player can do to practice hospitality toward those teams and players coming in next, or if it is the last game of the day, toward the host facility staff and maintenance crew?

BUILDING YOUR CHECKLIST
ANYTHING NEEDED? ANYTHING LEFT?

SPACE FOR OTHERS

CLEAN PLACES TO SIT

CRUMBS OR STICKY RESIDUE

PERSONAL BELONGINGS

EMPTY WATER BOTTLES OR WRAPPERS

Chapter 12

Finding the Camaraderie

I t's a group of people with only one thing in common: sports. At least at first. Whether it's a neighborhood, school, organization, or the world of travel sports, the challenge is still the same. How do you fit in? How do you get to know people? It may be simple in a group that easily stretches like putty to include newer members. Or in one that feels like a Wiffle[12] ball with its lightweight, perforated plastic shape allowing for natural and abundant movement. Here conversation flows, topics have lots of openings for participation, and the air feels as light as a feather. Other situations may feel like a baseball (compact, tightly woven seams in a cover as snug as a glove) with no way in or out.

As the Newbie

While communication and feeling welcome are often a two-way street, there are things you can do as the new family on the team:

- ➤ Cheer on all the team members
- ➤ Say "hi" and "bye" (avoid the temptation just to slip out and away)

➤ Shake hands with the other players and their families as you come and go

➤ Get to know the other families and players as you dust off your networking skills and learn new ones

➤ Do a deep dive into conversation starters (Debra Fine's book *The Fine Art of Small Talk*[3] has some great ideas)

➤ Observe and listen for things that could be safe conversation starters at other games

➤ Talk to the other new families on the team (especially about non-travel sports topics)

➤ Breathe

➤ Smile

DID YOU KNOW?

"Hello *is first recorded in the early 1800s, but was originally used to attract attention or express surprise ('Well, hello! What do we have here?'). But the true breakthrough for this now-common word was when it was employed in the service of brand-new technology: the telephone. Thomas Edison himself claimed to have initiated the use of* hello *upon receiving a phone call—which required people to address an unseen and unknown person. It was simpler and more efficient than some other greetings used in the early days of the telephone, such as 'Do I get you?' and 'Are you there?'"*[4]

If, at times, it seems like things are going nowhere, keep persevering. The season goes by fast but presents lots of opportunities. Give grace to others on the team. Be interested in others and be someone others want to know because they sense you care about them. Guard against taking things personally.

Everyone has things that are happening off the field, and it may have been a rough day before they arrived at the game. At times when I've gone to a game, the logistics of juggling everything just to get there, tense moments with family members, or the weight of a burden meant that I sat a little farther down the foul line to absorb the game for a bit (or at times, even the whole game) and get my focus back on track so I could talk and chat with other parents later. So, give everyone the benefit of the doubt, regardless of where they sit. And if they're farther down the sidelines—send them a bit of cheer with a smile and a wave, and then catch up with them after the game.

When You're One of the Established Ones
The process of getting to know the team is indeed a two-way street, though. If you're already established on the team, be proactive in expanding the circle, reaching out a hand, and helping new families feel welcome. The following ideas may seem like common sense, and you may already do a lot of them, but a reminder never hurts:

➤ Introduce yourself
➤ Say "hi" and "bye" to the new families
➤ Sit with someone you don't usually sit with
➤ Invite someone new to sit with you and others
➤ Include others with get-to-know types of questions and topics (without it sounding or feeling like an interrogation)
➤ Be conscious of whether the conversation is inclusive or not—notice someone's body movements and mannerisms (a huge home remodel may not be an ideal conversation starter for someone who is just scraping by to pay for baseball)

As parents gather and join teams for lunches, dinners, and post-game events, remember the ones who haven't shown up yet, the quieter ones, and the ones who aren't your best friends. Keep an open chair policy. Save the meal or gathering with a small group of your closest friends for a time when the invitation isn't open to the whole team and all parents. Embrace the concept of a team community. Get a slightly bigger table than you think you need when you are seated by the restaurant staff. Leave chairs open or space to add chairs easily. Sit or gather in a place that allows room for expansion without drawing attention. Think quickly with a smile.

If you are the one who is joining the party—breathe! Positively channel any awkwardness or embarrassment you may feel, rather than letting emotions unnecessarily lead you into an impetus fight or flight response you'll regret later. You never know what you might discover, the misconceptions that might be changed, or the new and surprising lifetime friends you might get to know from those shared experiences.

DID YOU KNOW?

The word 'goodbye' has its roots in shorthand, a phrase, and a 16th century English term. Interestingly, "this common farewell comes from the 16th century English term 'godbwye' which is shorthand for 'God be with ye.'"[56]

Regardless of where you find yourself on any given team, whether the newbie or the veteran, no one is perfect. And the process of communication isn't perfect either. Weave your strengths and personality style into the "Extending a Hand" checklist at the end of this chapter to flesh out this whole idea of camaraderie on the journey even more. Then give grace to one another, and as you do, you will be working together to travel the travel team circuit without *constantly* blowing a circuit.

Give grace to yourself too. Having a son or daughter play on a travel team is fun, but it can also be hard and exhausting at times. So even as you care for others, taking time for yourself is crucial. In the journey-maker space at the end of this section, jot down some of the hospitality highlights you've given and received so far, and then read on to discover some ways to take care of yourself too.

BUILDING YOUR CHECKLIST
EXTENDING A HAND

SMILE

GENUINE INTEREST

WHEREVER THEY SIT

TABLE AND CHAIRS

HELLO AND GOODBYE

Becoming a Journey-Maker:
Your Hospitality Highlights

Becoming a Journey-Maker:
Your Hospitality Highlights

Becoming a Journey-Maker:
Your Hospitality Highlights

PART V

Being the Best You Can Be

So far, a lot of the focus of this book has been about others. However, being on a travel team isn't just about your player, family, logistics, faith community connections, or hospitality. It's also about you. Not all families travel to games and tournaments as players get older, and high school age travel teams vary in their approach and philosophy regarding this. But for those moms and dads who do travel, being involved with a travel team can get tiring as you juggle schedules, relationships, and finances. It's easy to get worn out. Taking care of yourself so you can be the best you can be is just as important as everything else. Calling a personal time out gives you a chance to do a systems safety check, inspect for frayed wires, and reset your connections. It is part of what enables you to do everything else. And it all starts with keeping perspective.

Chapter 13
Keeping Perspective

E ven though you've watched many games, seen your son or daughter do thousands of practice drills, and know your son or daughter the best, they may still surprise you. The dropped pass, missed spike, or botched relay throw may not be what you have come to expect from your player and catch you off guard. Like moments in life, though, that play may not be the whole picture. The at-bat or failure to dig out a ball that didn't look so great from the stands may have some positive elements from the coach's or player's vantage point. And so, at that moment, and in the moments that follow, keeping perspective is crucial.

An "Ah-Ha" Moment

The concept of keeping perspective was brought home one day after a game in our early days of travelball when my son's at-bats had been inconsistent. And from my view in the stands, his pop-up was not helpful, and of course, I "knew" he could do much better. At least, that was my initial thought.

Yet during a conversation with my son later, I saw a different perspective. While my son knew the at-bat wasn't perfect, he also knew it was better—better because his technique had improved and because he'd made contact on the sweet spot of the bat. I had a choice to make. My son already knew what had gone right and what had gone wrong, and he had already talked with his coaches about it.

It was time to move on and focus on what he'd done right. Time to be positive rather than critical. Time to talk about something else besides baseball, or maybe not to talk at all. And time to give breathing room and space for rest and recovery, both physically and mentally, after an intense game. Keeping perspective was the right choice then and continued to be for good relationships and everyone's growth on our travel team journey.

DID YOU KNOW?
The odds of being left-handed: 1 in 10.[1]

"Enjoy the time you have with your kids because it goes by too fast," writes author and speaker Bill Severns on his website, keeperslegacy.org. Growing up, Bill played baseball with friends in what he refers to as the "sandlots" of the neighborhood, and continued playing in Little League, high school, college, and then professionally for the Brewers organization. When Bill and his wife had kids, the baseball journey picked back up once again as Bill coached his kids and their friends, aged five to seventeen, for twenty-two years. Today, Bill shares his passion for coming alongside parents and coaches in the legacy they are leaving on and off the field through his organization, The Keepers Legacy. While our exact responses in conversations with our son varied as we traveled the baseball journey, trying to keep an overarching positive attitude was always important to having the right perspective.

Extend that perspective beyond your player to the teams, coaches, and umpires. Just as a variety of factors influence a ballplayer's at-bat and defensive play, a variety of factors can influence a team's game performance and outcome.

Room for Learning

For coaches, their decisions before, during, and after games encompass many aspects. Yet, for a whole host of reasons, they may not be able to give you detailed reasons for every decision they make. Keep perspective. Think about your own life and responsibilities for a minute. Do you always explain everything you do to everyone? (The caveat here, of course, is if you are concerned about player safety or laws being broken.) With perspective, you may even decide that a conversation isn't necessary after all, recognize your player isn't concerned, or realize it's a later conversation for your player and the coach at the right time and place. If your player and coach need to have a conversation, talk with your son or daughter about it and be present as needed to give the gift of silent strength to support your son or daughter as you model respect for the coach

David encouraged his kids to talk to their coaches whenever possible. "I believe this taught our children to speak for themselves and establish a relationship with the coach," he says. He remembers one time when the coach moved his son from offense to defense. When his son was nervous about talking to the coach about his new role, David assured his son that he would be right there in the background if his son needed him. David remembers the confidence his son gained from a good interaction with the coach, the understanding his son gained after realizing why the coach made that move, and the opportunities that opened up for his son in skill areas and playing positions.

Approach coaches with an attitude toward communication, understanding, and the right time and timing, rather than challenging their decisions. Be intentional about learning. Be interested in getting to know who the coaches are as people, not just what they do as a coach.

When it comes to organizations, each has a unique philosophy and style that is reflected in its coaching staff, team policies, general procedures, and communication. Situations and context also impact the communication that leaders and coaches within the organization have with parents and players. And sometimes, those contexts and situations aren't related at all to the sport, team, organization, players, or players' families. Keep perspective. Coaches and leaders are people, too, and they often have things going on in their lives above and beyond their coaching duties. I remember once wondering why a coach wasn't replying to emails or texts. Later, I found out during a conversation with him that he was working multiple jobs and taking care of elderly parents.

DID YOU KNOW?
The odds of being a chronic procrastinator: 1 in 5.[2]

Even after your best efforts at researching, preparing, and planning before committing to a team, recognize that there may still be things to discover about the team, the organization, and the best fit for your family. Once your son or daughter is on a team and your family is part of the organization, be gracious in responding to the coaches and organization's level of communication. It may be like what you have already experienced from other coaches, teams, and organizations. Or it could be quite different. Be a student, be a learner, and try to avoid jumping to conclusions. (And yes, I know this can be hard at times, but it can be worth it in the long run.)

Communication styles and preferences can also be different from coach to coach within the same organization. Conversations at the field may not be the best time for some but perfectly OK for others, even if those conversations are not during a practice or game. Or maybe the coach isn't a "morning" or "late-night" person. Don't be afraid to ask coaches when the best time to contact them is. Find out how a particular coach likes to communicate, too. Is there a preference for in-person, phone, text, or email communication? If it's in-person, are there mannerisms that you can pick up on as you approach the coach to help you discern whether it is a good time to talk? Does the coach have stated rules or policies to help foster good communication?

In the book, *Travelball: How to Start and Manage a Successful Travel Team* by Ron Filipkowski, Ron talks about what he calls his "cooling off period" rule. He writes, "This rule is very simple—no parent is allowed to talk to me about these issues [e.g., player playing time] until twenty-four hours after the last game of a tournament."[3] He does this, he says, not just to give parents time to cool off but also for him to be able to have some quiet time after an intense tournament weekend and to be able to reflect on the tournament as a whole—its negatives and its positives.[4]

When Brian gets a call or message from a player's parent, he also has a twenty-four-hour rule. "More times than not, when they've had time to sit and think about it, they realize the issue that they're upset about is more their issue than their kid's issue," he says. "So, the twenty-four-hour rule and waiting are very important. And then when you do talk, respectfully communicate in a calm, easy manner. Talk to the coach about what your concern is and let him explain to you why he did things in a certain way."

Keep perspective. Your learning curve in this probably won't be perfect. I know mine wasn't. But the good thing? Learning is never static. There's always room for learning; it's something you can always be doing. And life often gives you a perfect opportunity in the very next moment to practice what you are learning. In one way or another, learning and the travel sports journey develop your character.

There are many, many travel organizations and teams in the United States. Be open to the best fit for your family. Look at the whole of the organization as much as its parts. At the same time, realize that you can't know everything about an organization or team before you start and that sometimes, you find out or see things you didn't expect as you are a part of it. The right choice (and sometimes most gracious choice) may be to change organizations or teams.

Maybe the organization or coach's communication style, approach, or philosophy isn't what anyone expected it would be or what you (or your player) want after all. The logistics might be too complicated on a variety of fronts. The supervision level might not meet your expectations. The playing schedule might be too much. The overall cost might be more than you anticipated, and it's just too much for your family. High entry gate prices (in addition to whatever the organization pays the tournament to participate in via player fees) for spectators at the organization's favorite tournaments might prohibit family and friends from attending. Your player might want a different playing challenge, tournament intensity, or coaching style due to changing interests. Your son or daughter may or may not be worried about being seen by recruiters or having a particular kind of travel team exposure for future opportunities.

There can be many reasons that expectations don't match a particular travel organization or team experience—and that isn't always a bad thing. If you choose to change teams or organizations, do it in such a way that isn't "team hopping." Make it about building the reputation of your family and player. Also, consider the timing of the change and, if at all possible, make any changes between seasons.

Back to Perspective . . . and Adding Grace

Having and giving perspective is about more than your player and the team's coaches. It's also about attitudes toward other players, other teams, other coaches, and tournament officials. Regardless of what organization or team you're with, at any given time the umpire's call you think is fantastic may not be going the other team's way. Be gracious. Maybe the other team is down ten runs. Be gracious. Or perhaps the team beating your son or daughter's team today has been the underdog over and over again, lost its last seven games, or been discouraged. Be gracious. Be proud of your team and show your excitement when something is going your way. Avoid those over-the-top reactions, though, that rub salt in the other team's wound as your team wins, and don't sulk when the other team wins. Graciousness in both situations goes a long way. Remember, the athletes on the field are eighteen and under. So are some of the fans in the stands. Just like you wouldn't take minors to a bar, don't take them to the spa of rudeness. Add compassion, grace, and discernment to your enthusiasm. And if your team happens to find itself in a losing streak, it will need encouragement and support more than ever.

"If I could instill in any parent just the overall sense of encouraging your kid and telling them how much you love watching them play, that's the biggest thing," Brian says. Let the coaches appropriately respond to the rough spots as you take the road of encouragement. "Enjoy watching the game because it's not a reflection on the parent. If your kid does bad or your kid does good, don't take credit for either one. Just watch them play and enjoy yourself. Let us [coaches] do our jobs," Brian says. Even the most challenging games have highlights to hold onto if you want to look for them and see them.

So, love the sport. At first, baseball wasn't my favorite game to watch. It seemed slow, it took too long, and I didn't know anything about the game. Yet, as my attitude became one of learning and embracing the opportunity, I developed an enjoyment of the sport, even when my kid wasn't playing in a specific game or particular inning. Find something to focus on during what may feel like a boring or tough game—even if it is just the weather, field location, or the design of the ballpark. At one game, I made up a silly, upbeat jingle that a fellow mom and I softly sang to ourselves at tough moments throughout the game. And since we were not packed in the stands like sardines in a can, it was easy to do discreetly—yet still very effective in continuing to love the sport, the game, and keeping a positive perspective in the moment.

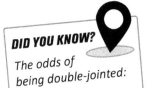

DID YOU KNOW?

The odds of being double-jointed: 3 in 100.[5]

Love the team too—the players, the parents, the coaches, the organization—whether it's a great game day or a challenging one. Cultivate a thankful attitude for people's efforts, regardless of how small or big those efforts are, even if you have to restart that cultivation multiple times within a single game. You never know what is happening off the field in coaches' or players' lives.

"You don't know if parents are struggling and could get a divorce, and they just had a horrible fight the day of the game," Brian says. "You don't know. So, encourage, encourage, encourage. And really focus on the other kids just as much as your own."

Think of the good in people. Just like a coach or player might have backup equipment in case something breaks, have a go-to backup perspective—something positive you can focus on that isn't dependent on people's actions, player performance, or game scores. Maybe it's a character quality of a particular player, a positive memory of the team, a favorite aspect of the organization you like, or just focusing on being glad to be breathing and alive to watch your son or daughter and the team do something they love. Or maybe it is simply a beautiful non-sports memory that changes your countenance and puts a smile on your face. And whether you tell people the reason for the smile—

well, that's up to you! The smile itself may be just what you and the people around you need to get back to loving the team during stressful moments.

After the Game

Keep the encouragement and positive perspective going after the game. When talking about the ride home in his blog post "Every Message You Send is Received," Bill says, "Tell your kids how much you love them and that you are glad that they are your kids and that you loved watching them play or perform."

Let your athlete be the guide on whether to talk about the game. "Just sit there and love on your kid and laugh and have fun. And if your son or daughter decides that they want to talk about it, they'll bring it up," says Brian. If your player does bring up the game, use discernment. "If you're going over every pitch and every play and everything, it eventually becomes like white noise," Brian says.

Avoid negativity, fault-finding, and blaming players, opponents, coaches, umpires, and referees. Instead, be part of building up the team, and indirectly, facilitating team bonding—something integral to a team's success. And if your player is quiet or brings up something that is seemingly off-topic, like where they want to go to eat—follow their lead and pick out a fun place to eat!

A Note about the High School Years

If your athlete is high school age, the perspective and gracious enthusiasm (and not being critical or complaining) you show as you watch the game also matters to other teams (players, coaches, families, and fans), game officials, tournament and facility staff, and any recruiters who are attending. Sometimes you can tell who the recruiters are, sometimes not. Sometimes the recruiter you see is a coach your player has reached out to, sometimes not. Keep perspective. It's a workday for recruiters and coaches who are there in a recruiting role, not a vacation day. They will be focused.

Yet even as recruiters and coaches focus on looking for specific things in players and on the field, they are very much aware of what is happening around them and what the parents on the sidelines are doing. They may or may not get a chance to talk with you or your athlete that day, but if they are interested in your player, they will be following up with your player and possibly your player's coach. If they are already talking with your son or daughter, they may also already be talking with the team's coaches. And as college coaches and recruiters observe players, the whole recruiting picture for them often includes the player's parents. What behaviors and attitudes do the parents exhibit in the stands? Is it positive? Is it supportive? Is it adding to or taking away from a good fan and game experience? What are they vocalizing that flies across fields and stadiums? What are they saying about players, teams, coaches, and umpires—quietly or otherwise? What interactions do parents have with their players, their players' teammates, and other parents?

During a recruiting process, the many conversations, interactions, and observations that happen before, during, and after games all have the potential to be part of the coach's internal discussions as recruiters and coaches look for the players who are the best fit for the school, the team, and position needs. So, yes, keep your composure and be cognizant of others during those high school travel sports years. Even more important, though, keep perspective and enjoy the game and each other—the years go by fast!

If you do have a conversation with a recruiter or recruiting coach, make it an effective one by (a) knowing the rules of contact ahead of time, (b) being polite, (c) paying attention to the recruiter's verbal and non-verbal cues, and (d) following their lead in how much time they have to talk. The National Collegiate Athletic Association

(NCAA) communication period guidelines are available on its website (www.ncaa.org).

Build a positive reputation for the team, as well as for your family and athlete, by keeping perspective and adding grace. Five questions to ask yourself before addressing an issue with a coach are the focus of this chapter's checklist. And during the moments when it's all about the umpires . . . well, there's a chapter just for them. Read on to find out why.

BUILDING YOUR CHECKLIST

KEY QUESTIONS TO ASK YOURSELF BEFORE ADDRESSING AN ISSUE WITH A COACH

IS IT AN EMERGENCY OR SOMETHING THAT NEEDS IMMEDIATE ATTENTION?

HOW MUCH TIME HAS ELAPSED SINCE THE ISSUE CAME UP OR THE SITUATION HAPPENED?

AM I CALM, THINKING CLEARLY, AND, AS MUCH AS POSSIBLE, KEEPING A POSITIVE ATTITUDE?

IF SOMETHING STILL NEEDS TO BE ADDRESSED, IS IT BEST FOR MY PLAYER, ME, OR BOTH OF US TO BE TALKING WITH THE COACH?

COULD THERE BE OTHER FACTORS AT PLAY THAT I DON'T KNOW ABOUT?

Chapter 14

When All You See Is Blue:
A Word about Umpires

A snapshot of any baseball moment reveals an array of color hues. Even the green of a grass field shades differently depending on the mowing pattern. But all the focus is on blue[1] when the crowd is reacting to an umpire's call. An umpire's view is not the view of the players, coaches, or fans—and vice versa. But why is this chapter here? You've probably attended lots of games already, so why do we need a chapter about umpires?

Our oldest son umpired baseball all through high school, so I have a special place in my heart for umpires. Over the years, I've seen all kinds of situations and behaviors from parents, fans, coaches, and players involving referees. And as we embarked on the travelball journey, umpires' skills varied, and the potential to disagree with umpire calls increased. Players' character that complements the game rather than disrupts it matters as much as their athletic skills.

Character matters for the fans too. Whatever the age of your son or daughter playing travel sports, well-chosen responses to the game and umpires from the stands and sidelines can be part of making it a great experience for yourself and others.

"If you get a bad call, it'll probably be made up just because of the nature of the way it [the game] goes," Bill says. "In a nine-inning or seven-inning game, you have lots of chances to win a ball game. The spectators aren't supposed to be the feature of the deal. So, enjoy the game. The umpires aren't usually trying to mess things up." As players get into high school, appropriate behavior from all becomes more and more important in the world of scouting and recruiting.

Staying with Perspective

So, keep perspective here too. Besides, the game is more enjoyable and healthier when your blood pressure is not too high! Umpires may have had a long day even before they got to the field for any number of reasons. Umpires may also end up calling many more games than they anticipated or be on the field longer than expected. The game load seemed to double for umpires at one of our tournaments due to weather which forced makeup games on the same day as the playoffs.

DID YOU KNOW?
Track and field referees include field judges, track judges, timekeepers, and starters.[2]

Yes, an umpire's job is to be professional—like all of us in our jobs—but umpires are also human. Anyone can have an "off" day. Extend grace. Keep perspective.

Give umpires and referees the gift of encouragement and a smile. For those doing the job because they love the game and love the kids, that gift keeps their passion alive for another day. For those who are umpiring gems (whether they do it because they love the job or need extra money), that gift keeps them coming back to umpire the next game. And for the umpire whose life has been hitting a rough spot, that gift can be one that calms and helps keep everyone going one more day.

As your son or daughter's character and athletic skills grow over the years, so can your responses and reactions to umpires as parents and fans. Be a model and example for your player and the rest of the team to follow in upping their game regarding umpire interaction and respect. Besides, you'll likely see the same umpires and referees again.

Build on Perspective

So, put people first, be an ambassador, and lead the way in your responses, not only to umpires and their calls but also in interactions around teams and coaches.

Putting People First

Umpires are human too. They have a job to do. Help make it a pleasant experience. Keep the fun in it for everybody. When Bill Severns umpired baseball one summer, he was fifty-three with forty-five years of baseball experience. Even with his experience and solid knowledge of the strike zone, umpiring was tougher than he expected.

He writes in *Keepers of the Sandlot*,[3] a book encouraging parents and coaches of Little League players to enjoy the game and the journey, "As Blue, I realized my imperfections and just how difficult the job was. I didn't need anyone in the stands aggravating that for me."

No matter which sport your athlete participates in, remember that the umpires and referees are people too. And as Bill puts it in his "Give up What's Holding You Back" blog post,[4] respond rather than "react" in anger. The players are soaking up everything like a sponge as they take in the actions they see and the words they hear. And as they do, they are learning life principles of how to treat others.

Being an Ambassador

Spread the goodwill. Represent yourself, your family, and the team well. Engage in self-monitoring with your verbal and non-verbal reactions. Cheer the team on, celebrate the good plays and right calls, and find the positive spin on plays that are riddled with errors and disagreeable umpire calls. Avoid insulting and name-calling.

Leading the Way

Be an example by being an ambassador and putting people first. Acknowledge the officials who are working hard, moving into positions to see plays, and being consistent with calls to both teams. When there isn't an opportunity to give immediate, positive feedback directly to those officials, be vocal with positive comments from the stands. Avoid obnoxious heckling of umpires and referees—even if you feel they could do better.

DID YOU KNOW?
Ice hockey has on-ice officials (including referees and linesmen) and off-ice officials.[5]

As for the players, remember, they're eighteen and under. Allow for context, compassion, and grace. It's a game. Be an encourager. Recognize good plays on your team and outstanding plays on the other team—it is possible to be an encouragement to any players giving their best effort. It is possible to encourage without disloyalty. You can say things like "solid block, catcher," "good stop, shortstop," "nice dig, setter," or "great job, goalie."

DID YOU KNOW?
Volleyball matches usually have two referees and two line judges.[6]

If even those words are hard to come by or you have to utter them through gritted teeth, try using the wonders of metaphors and similes to create fun visual images in your mind for enthusiastic cheers (even if you have to say them to yourself while you smile and clap).

Draw on the beauty of nature; words of literature (classics, kids' books, and nursery rhymes); superhero stories of old; and everyday objects to focus your mind and positively channel your thoughts. Here are some ideas for baseball. Add additional ideas in the margin, whether for baseball or another sport.

For the umpires:

- ➤ eyesight as sharp as a tack
- ➤ strike zone consistency as strong as concrete and as smooth as butter
- ➤ position moves that give right angles on the play
- ➤ squaring up behind the plate like they're in the center squares on a sheet of graph paper

For the catcher:

- ➤ arms like an octopus that reach high, low, sideways, back, front, and to the far corners to block and stop balls
- ➤ a springy body that jumps up like a jack-in-the-box to catch pop-ups
- ➤ feet that pivot as quickly as a well-greased swivel stool to go after wild pitches
- ➤ knees and joints as lubricated as a well-oiled machine for safe ups and downs
- ➤ a core as strong as a healthy tree trunk so muscles and limbs can do their work
- ➤ a neck that bends like a willow tree instead of staying stiff as a board
- ➤ a body that moves like an accordion to block pitches in the dirt
- ➤ cat-like reflexes for pickoffs that stop base stealing and get players out

For the infielders:

- ➤ standing tall like a giraffe or as if they were on stilts for that extra inch to catch those over-the-head balls

➤ a waist bending freely and arms moving effortlessly to drop down like low hanging fruit on a vine to block, stop, and scoop the ball

➤ legs that stretch like a rubber band to maximize reach

➤ feet that dance a jig or country two-step to the right base or place on the field before the ball gets there

➤ toes or feet that stick like honey to the base as the ball sinks into the mitt

➤ diving for balls with the precision of a synchronized swimmer

For the outfielders:

➤ running as fast as a cheetah to get those balls hit in the gap

➤ scooping and turning with the urgency of a farmer who is cultivating and planting fields before the storms come

➤ throwing to the cut-off guy with the speed of a supersonic jet and the accuracy of a surgeon

➤ like the infielders, diving for balls with the precision of a synchronized swimmer

If one of these doesn't help right away, forget about the previous play and look forward to the next one. And if you're still stuck, here are some other options I've found can work in the right circumstances: discretely take a walk; go to the concession stand; or head to the car to listen to music, read a book, run a quick errand, or do a work task. Avoid getting on social media to complain or getting immersed in things that would work against getting back on track with a positive attitude. (Plus, with the way comments on social media can go viral immediately, negativity on social media will not help you, your player, or the team!)

Once you've developed a supportive demeanor and mindset, head back to the game to enjoy the rest of it. (To make sure you're ready, consider using a checklist like the one coming up titled "Ready to Cheer." Ask yourself: Do I have kind words to say? Am I thinking positively? Do I appreciate the efforts?) Positive mental attitudes transform demeanors and help you keep positive perspectives not just on the umpires but also on parents, coaches, players, and the game.

BUILDING YOUR CHECKLIST
READY TO CHEER

KIND WORDS

POSITIVE THOUGHTS

BELIEF IN BEST EFFORTS

APPRECIATION FOR OTHERS

GOODWILL TOWARD PEOPLE

Chapter 15

Taking Care of Yourself

A s much as positive attitudes and interactions are important with players, coaches, families, and umpires, someone else is also important: you. With local teams and games, you'll spend a relatively short window of intense time with the team for each game. It is easy to get some space as everyone gets in their cars to go their separate ways home or on to other events and commitments.

In the Midst of the Season

With a travel team, where there is often extended time around people, it can sometimes be more challenging to find respite, reenergize yourself, and achieve the right balance of time around (and not around) people amid everything. But with a little creativity, it is possible to do all that without offending others. Here are seven ways to find respite:

1. Take a walk around the ballpark while the players are warming up.
2. If someone you trust can safely take your son or daughter to the field or players can travel to the field together, enjoy the break.

It'll give you time to spend some moments in quiet reflection, take a shower in peace, swim a lap in the hotel pool, or take a quick trip to the hotel weight room before heading out to the game.

3. If faith is a vital part of your life and who you are, be deliberate about setting aside moments to recharge, renew, and refocus yourself spiritually.

4. Check in with your faith community in some way—look back at chapter 9, titled "When Games Overlap with Your Church's Weekend Services," for ideas to refuel your heart, mind, and soul.

5. Vary the time you leave hang-out gatherings, so you are not always the last person there.

6. As your player gets older or if you start travel sports when your player is a high schooler, be your journey-maker too. Create your own special moments and memories that you will be able to look back on with a smile as the years pass.

7. Do something fun before or after games when your player is busy with the team. Immerse yourself in one of your favorite hobbies, start a new hobby, or do some sightseeing. Rest and relax with a favorite pastime. Do an exercise routine you enjoy. Splurge on an on-the-run spa appointment.

- Moms, if a spa appointment is out of your budget, not accessible, or not possible due to time or location, there is another option. Create a travel spa-on-the-run pack before you go out on the road or stop by the local grocery store at your destination for supplies for a personal spa treatment. There is an abundance of beauty books and articles on the market (online, at your library, etc.), and sometimes, even in the most unexpected places. An issue of *The Old Farmer's Almanac* includes an article titled "Beauty on a Budget" by Martie Majoros.[1] If you do create a personal travel spa-on-the-run pack (1) make sure the source is someone credible and trustworthy who you feel comfortable taking advice from, and (2) make sure that those ingredient and supply suggestions are medically safe and allergen-free for you before you use them.

And Even in the Off-Season

The need for respite, rejuvenation, and balance doesn't stop when the summer tournaments end. Sometimes the need for those things can even intensify in the off-season. In our first couple of years, we quickly discovered that we were not as prepared as we thought we were for the intensity of year-round baseball and travelball. As short August breaks in the world of travel baseball rapidly gave way to a combination of fall practices, fall tournaments, and winter off-season training, it did not take long for all that to catch up to us. (And especially me, since I did a lot of the driving to get my son to everything.)

No matter which sport your athlete plays, it's important to remember to take care of yourself in the off-season too. Your player is happily continuing to get to know teammates, strengthen athletic skills, and build opportunities during the off-season. But when your initial excitement about this new adventure wears off sooner than you expected or you suddenly find your enthusiasm unexpectedly wavering, it can catch you off-guard. And when weariness tiptoes in unnoticed, the build-up of fatigue may show itself in surprising ways and at unwelcome times.

Adding a school schedule back in after the summer on top of continued sports commitments (and any other ongoing volunteer, work, community, or family commitments you or your player have) may be more challenging than you thought it would be. If you are starting travel sports during high school and your son or daughter wants to play college sports, then the search for the right place to play athletics and earn a degree quickly adds another dynamic and time layer to an already busy schedule. Those are times when you need to remember that you are important, too, and find ways to make the journey work for the whole family—which may mean some give-and-take, compromise, and teamwork from everybody as you find ways to take care of yourself in this journey.

Sometimes the travel team, organization, and training facility are within walking distance or a short drive, which is great. A player of high school age with a driver's license may be driving to practices, games, or the training facility. For others, public transportation is close and easily workable. In our situation, while our son's first travel team was local with practices nearby, nothing was a close walk. The second travel team he played on was based out of and practiced at a facility in the area but was about an hour away in good traffic. With his high school team that traveled, those games were all over Illinois and near the Illinois-Indiana border on the Indiana side. As the first homeschool high school baseball team in Illinois, we were part of starting that team. It didn't involve a team bus. Families and players did the driving.

DID YOU KNOW?
Statistics indicate more than 4 million miles of roads crisscross the U.S.[2]

As the time I was spending on the road for sports and other family needs increased, it became apparent during one of our off-seasons that we needed to do something different. We didn't have another driver or vehicle yet, so we had to dig deeper and get more creative in finding solutions. For us, that meant a combination of my husband picking up more of the driving, organizing rides from others, looking into public transportation (while there was not a train station in our town, there were several in the area), and making schedule adjustments.

In addition to driving responsibilities, finances can be another area of stress that doesn't always get a break during the off-season. If you are doing monthly payments instead of a lump sum for off-season work as well as the upcoming summer travel season, it can feel like you just got done paying for one season when the time comes to pay for the next one. And it doesn't matter if those monthly payments are coming out of your pocket, your player's pocket, or some combination of the two—just the constancy of money always going out for travel sports with limited reprieve can wear on you and make you feel like you are in a pressure cooker. Taking care of yourself may mean finding ways to let the steam out of that pressure cooker.

Budgeting and a focus change-up are two tools that can help. Budgeting adjustments could involve revisiting the overall budget or looking creatively within a single paycheck's budget to make changes. Briefly tweaking the spending focus to something that is not required or sports-related could also make a difference and ease the pressure for a moment. Maybe it's a family Friday night ice cream or bowling outing with no travel sports talk. Perhaps it's the player spending a little bit of their hard-earned money on something they want rather than something that is required. The money doesn't stop going out but directing the money differently or taking some time for fun can relieve some stress.

Off-Season System Checks

Even in the off-season, step back and do a system check on three fronts: your player, the family, and you.

Your Player

Touch base with your son or daughter to make sure travel sports is still something he or she wants to do. The answer may still be an enthusiastic, resounding, whole-hearted yes. On the other hand, you may sense that there is a different answer your player doesn't know how to articulate or initiate expressing. Maybe interests have changed, travel sports is more work than anticipated, or it simply isn't fun anymore.

"As they get older, the funnel gets smaller," Brian says. "The competition gets harder, and the road to continue to play baseball becomes harder and more of a job versus just, you know, youth baseball having fun."

Whether the game is baseball or something else, the same principles apply in travel sports. So, reflect on the previous season or two during off-season checks. What negative or positive life and well-being changes have you noticed in your athlete's character, stress level, or relationships? What verbal and non-verbal indications give you insight into your athlete's thoughts about continuing with travel sports?

Your Family

Checking in with family is closely related to checking in with your player. Discuss whether travel sports is still fun and a good fit for your family. Revisit the reasons you started travel sports in the first place and make sure they are still valid or validate new ones. Reaffirm the decision. Or maybe even change your decision. In the earlier chapter about keeping perspective, part of the discussion touched on when it might be time to change teams or organizations. Keeping the fun in a travel sports journey, being a journey-maker, and traveling the circuit without *constantly* blowing a circuit is all about knowing when to keep going, how to keep going, and when to adjust.

The off-season can be an excellent time to reevaluate, think about adjustments for the season ahead, or maybe even make significant and unexpected changes that mean not continuing with travel sports—all of which are OK.

"And if your son, or daughter, decide they don't want to play, then forcing them to or trying to push them to play is doing them a disservice because now it becomes a grind for them and financially a grind for your family," Brian says. "And then you have the opposite side where somebody just really, really, really loves it, and they play for a long time."

When touching base with your player and your family, I wouldn't suggest doing this multiple times during the off-season. Nor do you necessarily have to do it *every* off-season—especially if your player is older. Also, not everything has to be a formal, sit-down, long, drawn-out conversation. (Even though I confess I am the one in our family who does like to have longer, sit-down discussions, so that has been an area I've been growing in over the years.) The player still needs to be able to focus and do the work of an athlete, and the middle of that work is not the time to sow any doubts. Give your son or daughter the space to be an athlete while you focus on just being observant and discerning. You can find out a lot by observing your player's interactions with coaches, family, friends, and teammates.

Create family times and memories during the off-season. Put in place special player and family traditions that only take place during the off-season. Involve the kids (no matter the age) in planning some parent-player and family days. The depth of the planning, logistics, and even the activity itself will vary based on the age of those who are involved in the planning and who will be participating in the activity. Starting early in involving others (even if it is just small steps) benefits everyone and is a process that can change and expand over the years as the kids get older. Mark those special days and traditions you are creating on the calendar in ink as soon as possible to show that those times are important family priorities, to help family members remember they are coming up, and to give everyone something to look forward to.

Brainstorm all-year traditions, too, during the off-season. Big or

DID YOU KNOW?

Eva Clarke from Australia recorded 3,737 pull-ups, the most pull-ups for a female in twenty-four hours, on March 10, 2016.[3] Brandon Tucker from Columbus, Georgia, recorded 7,715 pull-ups, the most pull-ups by a male in twenty-four hours, on October 26, 2019.[4]

small, the cost could be as little as free or something a bit more costly—whatever is in your budget. Maybe it's special outings with grandparents or extended family members. Perhaps local events become monthly or annual family traditions. A unique family hobby that interests everyone could also be an impetus for traditions. Or maybe it's a tradition that develops around road trips—whether those road trips are for sports or something else.

DID YOU KNOW?

The two national doughnut days are the first Friday in June and November 5.[56]

With a range of family interests, including sports tournaments, doughnuts were the first thing on Brian's family's agenda whenever they headed out of town during the year. "One of our traditions was that every time we would have to go on a road trip someplace, we'd always stop and get doughnuts for the ride," Brian says. "That was to set it off, that 'Hey, we're on a road trip and so we're going to stop and get doughnuts.' The kids loved it."

You

Take some time for yourself, too, as you do off-season system checks. If nutrition, exercise, and sleep fell by the wayside during the season, refocus on healthier eating, exercising, and sleeping habits. Take some time to personally evaluate and reflect in your own space, in the quietness of your heart and soul. It may be as simple as taking advantage of any calm and tranquil moments as you move from one thing to another or strategically setting aside a block of time just for you.

Ask yourself:

➤ Has more and more driving crept in unnoticed as time has gone on?

➤ Do you still enjoy the concept of travel sports and watching games, tournaments, and competitions?

➤ Are you still enjoying the rest of your life?

➤ Are you not enjoying other things in life anymore?

➤ Is your player enjoying life?

➤ Is each family member, and are you as a family unit, enjoying life?

➤ When was the last time you did something fun or non-travel-sports-related?

➤ When was the last time you did something fun or non-travel-sports-related as a family?

➤ Do you only see your player when you are driving somewhere together?

➤ If your player is older, are you managing more of the schedule than you realize or than you need to?

➤ How much of your focus is still travel sports-oriented, even though it is the off-season?

If the answers surprise you, maybe it's time to make some changes. In small or big ways, try expanding, eliminating, rearranging, consolidating, and grouping.

Consider grouping activities differently. For example, if your player has always volunteered somewhere on a specific day, could that be coupled with something else on another day to make logistics easier? If your player and any siblings work or volunteer at the same place (or nearby each other) and they will finish an hour apart, can one stay later so you can pick them both up at once? Or, if one of them has a driver's license, could they share a ride?

Consolidate activities, so you don't have to drive as much. For example, could your athlete walk or take public transportation to meet you somewhere to go to practice from a rendezvous point, rather than you driving to pick your son or daughter up and also driving to practice and then home?

"My daughter used to take the train into the city so I could drive her to dryland training," David says. "She would do her homework on the train. After practice, I would let her drive home since she had her permit and used the hour-ride home to meet her requirements for the test."

Eliminate time on the road whenever possible. While there wasn't a train station in our town, there were several stations in neighboring communities and one by the training facility. With help from my husband, the train, and a schedule adjustment, my driving time to take our son to practice was cut in half on some days. And it also gave my son another way to invest in the journey of travelball and be part of a group solution. Or, could your older player safely walk, ride a bike, or use public transportation to places and events instead of getting a ride from you?

Expand the solutions and the drivers. With a little bit of planning and looking at the schedule from a fresh perspective, we found different ways to change the driving situation for us. Look again at transportation issues and your carpooling options. With one team, I dropped my son off at another player's house to go with them. Consider expanding your options beyond parents if you have older players. Can your athlete meet teammates somewhere to get a ride? Can you work out finances for insurance or another vehicle? If another vehicle isn't possible, could a tweak in schedule logistics make the family car available for your player (who has a driver's license, of course) to drive to practices or games sometimes? Can siblings drive siblings? Could your son or daughter safely stay longer after a class, community, or volunteering commitment to study and wait for a ride from you or someone else? Can your player go to work with you or your spouse and then go to a practice or game from there? Sometimes expanding solutions means adjusting our paradigm and not always assuming your player can only leave from home or school to get to a practice, game, tournament, or training facility.

Sometimes in the off-season, just like during the playing season, taking care of yourself to be the best you can be is all about the simple things and remembering what gives you joy in any season. It's about coming full circle, back to the beginning of the chapter and those things you found respite in, reenergized yourself by, and achieved balance with during the playing season: exercise, quiet moments of reflection, faith-strengthening, hobbies, sightseeing, and yes, maybe even a spa splurge.

Think about where you are today in this imperfect adventure of travel sports that your family has undertaken. Use the "My Journey" checklist as a starting point. Expand the list to include areas that are important and unique to you and your situation. Then turn the page again to reflect on season highlights and good memories. What did you try for the first time, again, or differently that worked for you this season during your travel journey? What were some of your personal best moments during the year? What were some of your go-to favorites in being the best you could be? Jot them down in this section's journey-making space. After all, unless your player is a senior in high school or the last of your kids to play travel sports, there's probably another season just around the corner to get ready to be your best for. And if you are in that senior or final season, getting those memories on paper is something you'll always treasure.

BUILDING YOUR CHECKLIST
MY JOURNEY

HABITS: EXERCISE, NUTRITION, SLEEP, TIME SPENT DRIVING

TRADITIONS: SOMETHING OLD, SOMETHING NEW

FAMILY: MILESTONES, CELEBRATIONS, TRADITIONS, BEING PRESENT, ATTITUDES

PEOPLE: ENERGIZING, DRAINING

ON THE PERSONAL SIDE: REJUVENATION, RENEWAL

Becoming a Journey-Maker:
Your Best Moments

Becoming a Journey-Maker:
Your Best Moments

Becoming a Journey-Maker:
Your Best Moments

Reflecting on the Journey

The travel sports journey is multi-faceted for players, parents, and families. It is also a little bit different for everyone in its focus and how it's experienced.

As you've read this book, you've discovered ways to make the most of the journey from a parent's perspective. You may travel to all the games or only some of them. Your player may be an older elementary, a junior high, or a high school student. Siblings may or may not come along. You may have just one athlete or multiple athletes in the family. It may be an experience with your only child, your first, last, or anywhere between. Along the way, life and relationships may be as imperfect as the journey itself. It was for us. So, wherever you are (or think you might soon be) on this adventure of travel sports, may it be one filled with moments of hope and joy and one that you look back on with memories that make you smile.

There's still more to come here, though, so as you reflect on the journey, turn the pages for journaling and note-taking space. You'll find a special interview feature ahead, too, as well as appendices with even more ideas to travel the travel team circuit without *constantly* blowing a circuit.

Reflecting on the Journey

Reflecting on the Journey

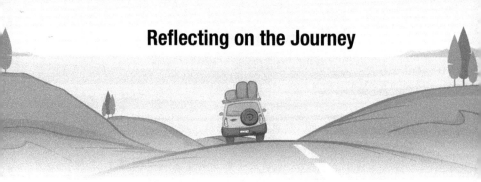

Reflecting on the Journey

Reflecting on the Journey

SPECIAL

INTERVIEW FEATURE

Behind the Scenes at Wrigley Field with Organist Gary Pressy

1,257–1,177–3
2,437

For Gary Pressy, those numbers aren't just any numbers. They are part of his personal Chicago Cubs history since he started playing the organ at Wrigley Field in 1987. And in early 2017 (just months after the Chicago Cubs became the 2016 World Champions), a phone interview with Gary was one of my delightful destinations in writing this book about travel sports. From statistics to favorite nuts, our conversation covered a wide range of topics, which are encapsulated below in this special feature.

That 2,437 number? As of January 31, 2017, Gary had played the organ for 2,437 consecutive games. The organ? A Lowrey. And the 1,257–1,177–3 number? It is the Cubs' win–loss–tie record at home from when Gary started in 1987 to February 15, 2017. Come with me now in this behind-the-scenes glimpse into Wrigley Field as we chat with organist Gary Pressy. Since equipment is a big part of baseball, the organ itself is where we start.

I asked Gary about the organs that have been part of the Wrigley Field experience.

This one [organ] is a Lowrey Heritage. It's been there since 2004, but it's got all the bells and whistles, and we keep improving the sounds and rhythms. We've been playing a Lowrey organ ever since there's been an organ at Wrigley Field. I've also played on a Lowrey Regent, and that organ was from 1997, I believe, to 2004. Great organ; great company.

We always try to add more rhythms to the organ to make different music changes. We try to change with the times also. So, in the off-season, we go down to the factory and implement new rhythms and substitute the old ones with the new ones. We put it on a disc, and then I put that disc in [the organ] before opening day and adjust all the different rhythms that we would want.

 What rhythms and sounds on the organ are the backdrop for what you add with the keyboard?

There are so many different ones we've implemented. There are marches and big band sounds. The disco sound is still there. The Lady Gaga dance is still there. Frank Sinatra is in there. Dixieland, Fox Trot, Hard Rock; introductions for *Pretty Woman*, *Beyond the Sea*, and *La Di Da Di*. The organ is more diversified [than a piano] as far as sound. An organ can have your piano, harpsichord, sax, clarinet, banjo, flutes, trombone, guitar, and more. Every once in a while, we like to just use the old, full organ sound. We try to implement something to please all the different fans we get.

♫ On the same tier as the TV and radio announcers (along with the public address announcer and the jumbotron operator), you and the organ are in a booth facing third base over by home plate. Has the organ always been there?

It's been there since 1989. In 1987, 1988, it was down the first baseline, and then they did reconstruction and put it down the third baseline.

♫ I've read in various articles that you started playing the organ when you were five years old. What did you love about the organ when you started playing it, and what do you love about it now?

I actually started piano for about six months, and I didn't find that as fun or challenging as an organ because of all the different sounds that an organ makes compared to the piano. So, I switched to the organ. My parents bought me a little Black Spinet organ, and I've been in love with the organ ever since. I've just always loved the organ sound. I would listen to ballgames on radio or TV and hear the organ in the background and say, "Boy, I'd love to do that someday."

♫ After taking lessons through childhood, you continued your music study beyond high school with private organ lessons. How do you keep up your skills today?

[In the early years] I had some great teachers guide me. I have a pretty good ear for music, which helps. My teachers would not like that sometimes because I would make up my own style, but I know my notes. Right now, everything is self-taught. I keep polishing my skills as I learn new songs.

Strong musical skills and what you refer to as "baseball judgment" have been key for you in successfully playing the organ at Cubs games. Tell us what you mean by baseball judgment.

There are many rules, like, when a pitcher is ready to deliver the ball, you cannot play. You try to implement songs [related to] what's going on in the field. You know, say, we're down 3-1, you'd want to play something that says let's go, let's pump it up, let's keep going. You've also got to be able to be spontaneous—you can't be fumbling over music sheets if something happens. Having a good ear helps with that. And you really have to be a baseball fan (or, if you're playing hockey, a hockey fan, whatever it is) and know the game. You can't go in there "cold turkey" because then you create a lot of problems.

How do you find songs to add to your repertoire?

I listen to the radio, or TV, and the Top 40. If I hear something I like, I learn it and add it on.

Playing the organ and being a baseball fan does not stop when the season ends for you. In addition to researching trivia for the scoreboard during games, you also do work for the Lowrey Company and are an enthusiastic participant in the annual Cubs convention in the Chicago area.

At the Cubs convention, they have clinics going on and meetings with the players that fans can attend, and I'm there entertaining right in the lobby. The fans will come up to me and ask me to play "Take Me Out to the Ballgame" or whatever they want to hear. It's the dead of winter, usually snowy, and ten degrees. And we're talking baseball, and that's great. They'll come up and say things like, "You know, I was at the game on July 3, and you played this or that, and that was pretty clever." And that's pretty priceless. You get to interact with the fans. Once I'm at Wrigley Field, I really don't, because I go up to my office and stay there.

It's an honor for me to be working for the Cubs, the organization, and I think it's priceless when people come up to you and compliment you on your work. It's neat to be a part of the convention, especially because it's during the off-season when there are no games.

As far as Lowrey, I do work for them in sales and demonstrating. Around the holidays, I'll play at luncheons for folks, and we'll have questions and answers. Sometimes I'm involved in doing concerts too. It keeps me involved with the Lowrey people, and as far as the convention, it keeps you involved with the Cubs fans.

♫♫ **Does the off-season work you do with Lowrey and at the Cubs convention help give you an ear and an eye for who the fans are and what they might want to hear? Does it help you in knowing what songs to add to your repertoire? Does it give you a feel for where the audience is and what they are interested in?**

Definitely. We get all different walks of life coming to Wrigley Field. Cubs fans are all different ages—from five all the way to eighty, eighty-five, ninety.

♫♫ **Cubs fans are known for their enthusiasm, loyalty, and devotion. Tell us about the Wrigley Field audience and moments of the 2016 World Series that stood out to you on the Cubs' way to becoming the 112th World Champions.**

The Cubs fans are people that if there are fifteen games left and you're thirteen games out, we're not out of it. And then sometimes they are people that if the glass is half-full or half-empty, when is it going to spill. But the fans are die-hards. They just don't say quit—no quitting in those crowds.

One of the most emotional games of the 2016 playoffs was Game 6 of the National League Championship Series with the [Los Angeles] Dodgers at Wrigley Field because that was the story right there to get to the World Series. I think the biggest game of the whole scenario, though, was the fourth and deciding game in San Francisco [against the Giants at AT&T Park—now called Oracle Park—during the National League Division Series]. We came back in the ninth inning, and I believe we scored four or five runs to win the game. Otherwise, we would have had to have brought the series back here for a do-or-die showdown, and who knows what would have happened.

As far as the Cubs at Wrigley Field, I think the atmosphere of Games 3, 4, and 5 of the World Series win it or lose it, and we lost two out of the three, but still wound up winning it. And I think in that Game 5, the fans had a sure thing that they were going to win. They weren't going to let this baby end that night. They were the tenth player. They really, you know, charged it up. They did their jobs, and so did the Cubs.

🎵 **Whether it is the iconic Ivy Wall, devoted fans, live organ music, the age of the ballpark, the "W" flag flown after wins, or the "Go, Cubs, Go" song, tradition is a key part of Wrigley Field even as renovations are underway and modern updates like the jumbotron have been added to the ballpark. Talk about the tradition you see at Wrigley Field.**

I think Wrigley's different. With the Cubs, you've got your parents, your grandparents, who will take you to the game. You've got the ivy. Outside sunshine most of the time for a day game, hopefully. Wrigley Field has such a tradition, and I'm so glad to be a part of that. It's the second oldest ballpark around, and we've implemented a few new things, but it's still *the* ballpark—the cathedral of all ballparks. You still have people working there from thirty to forty years ago, and they keep up traditions and interact with the younger people who may be in a position of work at Wrigley Field also. It's when your grandparents would take you to the game, and you'd see Ernie Banks, Ron Santo, Billy Williams, and even further back than that, and then you go into a different era with Bill Buckner in the '70s. You've got people who went to games in the 1940s at Wrigley Field.

 What is your pre-game prep?

On game day, I get there about three hours before the game, have lunch or dinner, get the songs ready, and then, about two hours before the game, start playing for about an hour. Between games, I follow baseball news on the TV, the internet, and the morning papers—keeping up on trades, players, teams, who's winning and losing, and just being a baseball fan.

 You've been playing the organ at Wrigley Field for a long time. What do you think has contributed to your longevity in this job?

Having a large library of music, good health, being knowledgeable as a baseball fan when playing the organ, and dedication.

 What do you think the organ music adds to the whole Wrigley Field experience?

A feel-good throwback as people walk in the stadium. Throughout the game, it's [the organ music] a great combination of old and new, of tradition and modern. It's a subtle invite to what was and what is.

1,411–1,273–3
2,687
33

In 2019, Gary announced his retirement from the Cubs following the year's season. He had been the organist at Wrigley Field for 33 years when he retired in 2019. That 2,687 number? As of Gary's retirement and last regular-season game on September 22, 2019, he had played the organ for 2,687 consecutive games. And the 1,411–1,273–3 number? It is the Cubs' win–loss–tie record from when Gary started in 1987 to the end of the regular 2019 season. Thanks, Gary, for being such a vital part of the organization, as well as the team and fans' Wrigley experience for so many years!

ABOUT GARY

Born: Brighton Park (Chicago)
Grew Up: South Side of Chicago
Attended: St. Laurence High School, Chicago (graduated 1975)
Lives In: Palos Hills, Illinois
Sang: During the seventh inning stretch in 2016 to mark his 2,400th game at Wrigley Field
A Baseball Fan: For more than fifty years
Favorite Concession Food: Hot dogs and hamburgers
Favorite Nuts: Lightly salted Planters brand cashews
Favorite Songs: "Hey, Hey, Holy Mackerel" (the Cubs fight song) and "Hot N Cold" by Katy Perry
Favorite Sponsored Events: Hockey games, conferences, concerts ("The Billy Joel and Elton John concerts were unbelievable," he says.)

ABOUT WRIGLEY FIELD[1][2]

Seating Capacity: 41,160
Built: 1914 (second oldest ballpark in the Majors)
Original Name: Weeghman Park
Previous Buildings on Property Include: A seminary
Scoreboard: Constructed in 1937 (original still intact)
Ivy: Purchased and planted by Bill Veeck in 1937
Lights: Added in 1988
Third Base Concourse Elevator: Added in 1996
Wrigley Field Is Also Known As: The Friendly Confines
First Team to Play Organ Music: 1941[3]

Acknowledgments

J ust like our family's travel sports journey, this project, too, has been an adventure. Life, with all its ups and downs, swirled around the days and months (and dare I say it, even a year or two!) of the path to publication. Many have been a part of the journey with me, whether they shared our travelball experience, encouraged my writing, believed in this book, or shared their sports stories with me.

My heartfelt appreciation goes out to my fellow journeymen and women, regardless of their athlete's sport, who offered their perspective and shared some of their travel stories with me. I'm grateful to Brian Holman, Gary Pressy, and Bill Severns for their willingness to be interviewed for the book. The abundance of time and insight they so graciously gave was a tremendous blessing.

I also want to thank the Write-to-Publish conference, faculty, speakers, writers, and editors. Many people and opportunities come to mind as I reflect on my experiences attending over several years, and I am grateful for all of them. I especially want to thank Cindy Sproles, one of the editors I met at that conference the first time I attended. She heard my heart and dream for this book and was steadfast in her encouragement (and prodding!) along the way. Write-to-Publish is also where I first talked to the EMoon publishing team. Thank you for seeing this book's vision and helping to make it a reality.

To family and friends who supported me along the way, thanks for believing in me and this project. And to the baseball players and families with whom we traveled, laughed, and learned, it was quite a ride! Thanks for being on the journey with us.

Finally, and most of all, thank you for investing in this book and using it to create a treasure to pass on from generation to generation. May it truly be something that sparks joy and holds good memories for years to come.

About the Author

S ue Rosenfeld was involved in the sports world for more than ten years as a parent, fan, umpire's mom, coach's wife, and athletic director's wife. She and her husband Dave have three sons. During their youngest son's high school years, they added another sports role—a travel baseball family. It's from those travelball years that this book project came.

Sue developed her journey-making passion and expertise from her family's sports experience, as well as her time spent in jobs, volunteering, and homeschooling. As an author and copywriter, Sue has worked with clients and editors on a variety of projects for more than twenty-five years. Her body of published work is both digital and print and includes press releases, website copy, eNewsletters, book contributions, and articles. In addition, Sue has a bachelor of science degree in occupational therapy; achieved her DTM as a member of Toastmasters International; and is a certified trainer in the Maxwell DISC Method.

Appendix A
Packing the Sibling Activity Bag

○ Sketchbooks and pencils for drawing

○ Coloring books

○ Origami papers and origami idea books

○ Paper and design books to make paper airplanes

○ A yo-yo

○ Note-cards to write and send to relatives

○ A deck of cards

○ A book on learning how to play solitaire
   and its many versions

○ A chess, checkers, or backgammon set

○ Travel games

○ Books to read

○ Schoolwork

- ◯ Flashcards
- ◯ Portable electronic games
- ◯ Tablet/iPad
- ◯ Toy cars
- ◯ Music instruments
- ◯ Music books
- ◯ Hand-held puzzles (e.g., mazes, sliders, cubes and other 3-D shapes)
- ◯ Sticker books and play boards (e.g., the Melissa & Doug company product line includes "Puffy Sticker Play Sets")
- ◯ Various sports balls, frisbees, compact outdoor games, etc.
- ◯ Outside exploration and discovery tools (e.g., a magnifying glass)
- ◯ Anything your kids are interested in, have as a hobby, or are passionate about doing and learning
- ◯ Ideas, resources, and supplies to safely practice world record attempts (learn more at the end of Appendix B)

Appendix B

71 Things to Do in an Hour

Whether it's sunny and over ninety degrees, overcast and cool, or raining a steady drizzle, the practice goes on and on. And even with the best phone weather apps, an unexpected bolt of lightning or rain turning dirt to mud and puddles to ponds can bring the game to a sudden stop until it's safe to be outside again, the field is playable, or the game is canceled.

So, you wait.

In the world of travel and tournaments, that wait time can become exponentially multiplied. Yet, it doesn't have to be annoying or wasteful; it can be an opportunity. It can be a time to have fun, accomplish tasks, rest, exercise, and be inspired. One player's mom put together flowers for her daughter's wedding while she waited. I wrote part of this book while I waited. I've developed speeches, written articles, taken naps, corrected schoolwork, practiced music, and read while I've waited. So, check out a stack of books from the library before you go, take some long-forgotten projects off your shelves at home, plan to slide in some work moments, or get creative with your location when you arrive.

At the Field
When it's just you:

1. Read a book
2. Read a magazine
3. Read a newspaper
4. Listen to an audiobook
5. Listen to a seminar or workshop recording
6. Study for a class you are taking
7. Do an independent course study
8. Attend a webinar
9. Listen to music
10. Work on a craft or sewing project
11. Take a nap
12. Take a walk
13. Write a speech
14. Practice a speech
15. Correct homework
16. Create lesson plans
17. Write a work report
18. Do a work conference call
19. Build relationships by talking with other moms and dads at the field
20. Research a book you are writing
21. Catch up on personal phone calls
22. Get caught up on political news
23. Study a second language
24. Practice sign language
25. Compose a song
26. Write a poem
27. Study the Bible
28. Tackle your email inbox

29. Proofread a document for school or work
30. Sketch a drawing
31. Write a letter

When you have your player's siblings with you:
32. Memorize Bible verses together
33. Help them memorize math, history, or science facts
34. Help them with homework
35. Play soccer, catch, Frisbee, or a lawn game
36. Practice music
37. Learn and sing some of the classic hymns
38. Read a book aloud
39. Hang out with families who have their kids with them
40. Talk to each other—practice the fine art of conversation
41. Make up stories and have a storytelling session
42. Take a walk

When you're with your spouse:
43. Talk to each other—practice the fine art of conversation
44. Catch up on the calendar for the week
45. Plan a family vacation
46. Pray together
47. Do a Bible study together
48. Listen to music together
49. Take a walk, go to a park
50. Work on projects independently

Back at Home
When you're close enough to go home:
51. Wash, dry, or fold a load of laundry
52. Exercise

53. Iron shirts
54. Send emails
55. Vacuum and dust the living room
56. Pick vegetables or fruit from your garden
57. Create fresh flower arrangements with flowers from your garden
58. Do a section of the cross-stitch, quilting, or sewing project you're working on
59. Fix a casserole or load up the slow cooker for dinner
60. Walk the dog or play with the cat
61. Feed the fish

In the Area

62. Run errands
63. Hang out at the nearest coffee shop
64. Go antiquing
65. Visit a museum or historical site
66. Play a round of miniature golf

From the Hotel

Incorporating a team and baseball focus when players need something to do:

67. Play a baseball video game
68. Go on a behind-the-scenes tour at a local ballpark or a local college or university's athletic facilities
69. Find an indoor training facility to practice hitting and fielding
70. Take advantage of local fun, such as miniature golfing and a beach day as a team
71. Go out to breakfast, lunch, or dinner as a team

You (or anyone along with you on the journey) could even practice for making or breaking a world record while you're waiting! *Guinness World Records 2017* includes a "Do Try This at Home" section. While the section is broken down by location (kitchen, backyard, bedroom, and gym), many of the ideas apply to a range of ages and can be portable to practice on the road during the travel sports journey. The *Guinness World Records 2019* "Do Try This at Home" features crafts, and in *Guinness World Records 2020* you'll find "Do Try This at Home" ideas in its "Viral Sports" section So, check out the ideas in the *Guinness World Records* books (or online at their website, guinnessworldrecords.com), and give one or more of them a try—keeping safety as a priority, of course!

Appendix C

A Personal Study

Sanctuary Required?: Faith and Life
Considerations in the Travel Sports Journey

Travel sports can mean lots of hours on the road, including Sundays. Integrating church and faith with a travel sports journey when games overlap weekend worship services was the focus of chapter 9 in this book. If you are wrestling with these issues, though, or are curious about what the Bible has to say on the topic of Sundays and church, the following study is designed especially for you. As I studied the question of "Sanctuary Required?" and then developed and wrote this part of the book, I also gathered insights from my husband David Rosenfeld, so you will see him quoted in the study. You can learn more about Dave, and his theology background, in his bio at the end of the study. After the study, there's still more to come, including fun chapter notes and a smorgasbord of baseball trivia!

What time is it? Are we there yet? Can we play now? Generation after generation has asked these familiar questions. Today, those questions take on an added dimension in the world of sports and travel teams. Decisions around practices, games, and tournament travel on Sundays can be challenging ones. Does a Christian have to be in a church building and sanctuary for a worship service with other Christians every weekend? How does the availability of church services on the internet (live and recorded) impact any questions you have and the decisions you've made or are making? Or, to put it another way—"Sanctuary Required?"

~ Beginning to Ponder ~

Asking the question "Sanctuary Required?" is designed to be a springboard for family discussion and reflection. In incorporating the Bible, the study does look at the topic from a Christian perspective; however, the reflection space and question prompts would be applicable for anyone actively involved in a faith community who has closely held tenets of faith that are integral to their life. So also are the family and life aspects pondered at the end of the study. The question "Sanctuary Required?" truly is multi-faceted.

Our sports story started in the years when stores closed on Sunday and organized sports usually took a break that day. Growing up, intramural soccer games for me (and baseball games for my husband) were usually held on Saturday, and we practiced during the week. Although my husband remembers one special weekend tournament, it was a rare occasion that would find either of us on a field on Sunday. We were able to attend church and be actively involved in our church community without it competing with playing sports.

When our boys first started playing sports, coaches primarily reserved Sunday for rainout makeup days. Over time, Sunday became not just a rainout makeup option but a common day for practices and games. As "travel sports" gained popularity, and tournaments became more of a business, tournament organizers began having playoffs on Sundays. And now, Sundays are the norm.

Think about your sports background and experiences (growing up and now; on Sundays and in general). Write some of those in the space below.

_____

_____

_____

_____

_____

Now take a snapshot of life today and your dreams of the future. In the space below, jot down some ideas and thoughts as you reflect on the following areas:

Lifestyle priorities:

_____

_____

_____

_____

_____

Family values:

_____

_____

_____

_____

Personal, player, and family hopes, dreams, and goals:

_____

_____

_____

_____

_____

Memories to keep and memories to build:

_____

_____

_____

_____

_____

Faith community beliefs and priorities:

_____

_____

_____

_____

_____

Additional thoughts:

_____

_____

_____

_____

~ Lingering in the Long Answer ~

The pondering has started. Leave those thoughts where you wrote them for now. It's time to dig deeper. The study that follows is not designed to tell you what to do or to be all-inclusive. Instead, it is a place to begin—a place to hit pause and linger for personal study, quiet reflection, and conversational side streets with family members. Come. Stay awhile. Discover. Journey. Find the gems for you.

For our purposes, asking "Sanctuary Required?" leads to a specific and focused question: Does a Christian have to be in a church building sanctuary every weekend to meet with fellow Christians for a worship service to worship God? A logical first step in exploring this question is the Bible's Ten Commandments (Exodus 20, Deuteronomy 5). Is there a verse there that answers this particular and narrowly focused question? The short answer is no. The longer answer is that the Bible does have a lot to say about the question "Sanctuary Required?" with several verses speaking to the question (Hebrews 10:23–25, Acts 20:7, and Psalm 95:1–7 are three foundational ones).

Identify the Presuppositions

Amid busy lives, we often don't take time to put words to the beliefs behind our ideas, concepts, thoughts, and opinions; they just are. Yet our tomorrows are impacted by today, and our todays are impacted by our yesterdays. What is influencing your assumptions? What are those assumptions? Take a few moments in the space below to bring those assumptions to the surface and put words to some of your pre-suppositions.

What do you think of when you hear the words: "sanctuary," "church," and "worship"?

Sanctuary:

_____

_____

Church:

_____

_____

Worship:

_____

_____

Now that you've put those presuppositions on paper, leave them there. They will still be there at the end of the pathway you are forging when you can decide whether to keep them, but for now, give yourself the freedom to discover.

All about the Words

As with all questions and answers, the words matter. For the question, "What do I do about Sunday church services, and do I have to be in a church building sanctuary every weekend to meet for a worship service with other Christians?" we're going to study the words "meet," "church," "building," "worship," and "Sunday services."

Meet

Look up synonyms for the word "meet" in the dictionary, and you'll see "assemble," "gather," and "congregate." In those synonyms, we find Hebrews 10:23–25. Read the three verses below from Hebrews 10 and then answer the questions.

> [23]Let us hold fast the confession of our hope without wavering, for He who promised is faithful; [24]and let us consider how to stimulate one another to love and good deeds, [25]not forsaking our own assembling together, as is the habit of some, but encouraging one another; and all the more as you see the day drawing near.

1. What does verse 24 tell us to stimulate one another in doing?

2. What comes to mind when you read the words "love" and "good deeds" in verse 24 in the context of the "assembling together" focus of verse 25?

3. What words in the second half of verse 25 give instructions about the meeting together/assembling?

4. Is there a specific day, time, or place for meeting mentioned in these verses?

5. What phrase toward the end of verse 25 identifies the frequency of the meetings?

Reflection Moment

Use the space below to write (in your own words) the principle(s) you've discovered about Christians meeting from studying Hebrews 10:23–25.

Hebrews 10:23–25 gives us baseline principles; other verses give us details of what took place when Christians met, assembled, gathered, and congregated. Study the verses below to observe (*a*) examples, (*b*) patterns, and (*c*) what is and isn't being said. Annotate each verse in the space below with the activities, time/day, frequency, and places mentioned.

Acts 2:42: _____

Acts 11:26: _____

Acts 20:7: _____

1 Corinthians 10:16; 16:2: _____

1 Timothy 2:8: _____

Ephesians 5:19: _____

Colossians 3:16: _____

What pattern do you see? _____

_____

_____

What isn't being said? _____

_____

_____

What is being said? _____

_____

_____

Reflection Moment

Where do you meet with other Christians now? What is part of those meetings (fellowship, giving, prayer, singing, the Lord's Supper, teaching, worship)? Write, draw, or sketch in the space below to symbolize your thoughts on this.

Reflection Moment

Now brainstorm additional ways to gather with other Christians and those in your faith community. Think about the large and small groups already in place that you are not a part of but could be. Think of new ideas and ways to explore keeping your fellowship with other Christians strong. Write, draw, or sketch in the space below to symbolize your thoughts.

Conversation Ready

Identify the key points from this section to discuss with your family member(s) and which family member(s) you hope to engage in that discussion.

Church

Phrases like "church building" and "going to church" are often used interchangeably with "church." Drive down the road, and you'll see steeples, crosses, and the word "church" on an abundance of buildings. So, where did the term "church" come from?

"The word 'church' first appeared in the New Testament. Jesus was the first one to use the word (in Matthew 16:18) when talking to Peter about the church that was to come after Jesus' death and resurrection," says Dave Rosenfeld, Diploma in Bible Theology, BS, MDiv, STM. "The Greek word at the heart of 'church' in the Matthew verse is the word *ekklesia*. Used over one hundred other times in the New Testament, the focus of *ekklesia* is on the idea of an assembly or gathering of people."

As the body of Christ (Ephesians 1:22–23), the church has both a universal (1 Corinthians 12:13) and a local meaning. "The church is comprised of all believers—past, present, and future," Rosenfeld says. "The Apostle Paul frequently talked about the local church, as he established many of them during his missionary journeys." Examine the passages below from the book of Acts and answer the corresponding questions.

Acts 9:31

[31]So the church throughout all Judea and Galilee and Samaria enjoyed peace, being built up; and going on in the fear of the Lord and in the comfort of the Holy Spirit, it continued to increase.

Where was the church?_____

_____

What were they enjoying?_____

_____

What was being built up?_____

_____

What was increasing?_____

_____

Acts 16:5

> [5]So the churches were being strengthened in the faith,
> and were increasing in number daily.

What was being strengthened? _____

_____

What were they being strengthened in? _____

_____

What was increasing? _____

_____

(Note: the word "number" refers to believers, or Christians.)

Reflection Moment

Ponder how your thinking of the word "church" may have changed with what you've read and studied in this section. Write, draw, or sketch in the space below to symbolize your thoughts.

Conversation Ready

Identify who you will talk to in your family about what you've reflected on and write that person's name here. Add notes about what you will share with them.

_____

_____

_____

_____

_____

Building

If the word "church" is about people, then where do buildings come in? Today, people and buildings are often intertwined in a faith community. But were they in biblical times? We'll study some physical structures the Bible mentions in just a bit, but first, let's look at the word "building" itself. Study the verses below to see key uses of the word.

In 1 Corinthians 3, the apostle Paul is writing to those in the city of Corinth (vv. 1–3). Look at 1 Corinthians 3:9 and list the three ways Paul describes people and who he is describing in the three phrases he used.

> [9]For we are God's fellow workers; you are God's field, God's building.

_____

_____

_____

Read Ephesians 2:11–22. Look especially at the last four verses (vv. 19–22). Write down how the concepts of building as a noun and building as a verb are used in these verses.

> [19]So then you are no longer strangers and aliens, but you are fellow citizens with the saints, and are of God's household, [20]having been built on the foundation of the apostles and prophets, Christ Jesus Himself being the corner stone, [21]in whom the whole building, being

fitted together, is growing into a holy temple in the
Lord, [22]in whom you also are being built together into
a dwelling of God in the Spirit.

_____

_____

_____

What visual picture came to mind as you pondered these verses and
the building analogy in reference to God's people? Describe or draw
it below.

So, if churches are about people and the word "building" is used
as an analogy for people, then where does our contemporary use
of "church" as an organization and the term "church building" come
from? Is there a biblical precedent for people gathering in places to
worship and hear God's Word taught? Find out by unscrambling the
crossword puzzle clues and filling in the puzzle. Look up the Scripture
verses referenced for context.

Crossword Puzzle

ACROSS

1. TBRNCLAEAE
Exodus 25:9; Exodus 35:10–19; Numbers 7:1

2. YNSGGAOUE
Matthew 4:23; Acts 13:14ff; Luke 4:14–15

3. TNTFMTNGEOEEI
Exodus 33:7; Leviticus 1:1; Joshua 18:1

4. TMPLEE
(also referred to as "house for the name of the Lord")
1 Kings 8:12–21; 1 Chronicles 29:1; Acts 2:46; Psalm 11:4;
Psalm 27:4; Mark 14:58; Luke 23:44–46; John 2:19;
Matthew 21:12–13; Mark 13:1–3

5. SNCTRYAUA
Exodus 25:8; Hebrews 9:1; Psalm 150:1

DOWN

1. HSSOUE
Luke 5:18–20; Mark 2:1–5; Acts 2:46; Acts 20:7–12;
Romans 16:3–5; Colossians 4:15; Philemon 1:2

2. BLDNGSUII
Acts 19:9

3. TDRSOUOO
Luke 5:1–14; Acts 16:13; Acts 17:22ff

1H
2S N A G E
1T 2B R N C E
U S
PLACES
I
3T N 3O F E T N G
U
S 4T M P E
O
R
5S A N T R Y

The tent of meeting is often described in the Bible as a structure the Israelites set up at specific times and for specific reasons during their years of wandering in the wilderness. Likely constructed around 1442 BC, the building of the tabernacle followed in 1440 BC.

> *"Both the Tent of Meeting and the tabernacle were designed as mobile structures so that when God instructed the Jewish people to move, they could pack up the structure and reassemble it in their new location—thereby enabling them always to have a place to worship God wherever they went,"* Rosenfeld says.

Proclaiming God's Word took place in a temple, synagogues, and houses—the physical structures of gatherings for hearing, studying, worship, and fellowship.

> *"King Solomon was tasked with building the first temple. He completed it in approximately 970 BC. Destroyed by the Babylonian King Nebuchadnezzar in 586 BC, the temple was rebuilt by the Jewish people returning from their exile in approximately 516 BC. This second temple stood during Jesus' time on earth—until it was destroyed by the Romans in AD 70. This is the temple mentioned in Acts 2:46 and other places in the New Testament. Between the Old and New Testament times (approximately 400 BC–4 BC), the synagogue was the main place where the Jewish people gathered for prayers, instruction about the Law, and worship. Both men and women attended their local synagogue, along with those not Jewish (known as Gentiles) who wanted to know more about the God of the Jews. The use of synagogues for this purpose was still prominent in Jesus' time, as is evidenced by*

how frequently the gospel writers mentioned the synagogue in their books," Rosenfeld says.

As the crowds grew, people packed houses (Luke 5:19) and listened to Jesus teaching outdoors (Luke 5:1).

Tents, tabernacles, temples, synagogues, houses, and outdoor gatherings were all precursors to our "church buildings." And it was in that New Testament sharing of the gospel and the events that followed that we have the roots of church leadership and organization—after Jesus' death, resurrection, and ascension when the gospel was being spread out from Jerusalem to Judea, Samaria, and beyond (Acts 1:8); as the number of converts to Christianity was increasing; and for the teaching, shepherding, and equipping of new believers (Ephesians 4:11–12; Titus 1:5; 1 Corinthians 14:40).

Summarize what you have learned from what you have studied so far in this section. What do you know now that you didn't know before?

_____

_____

_____

Reflection Moment

What has impacted you the most in this part of the study? Write, draw, or sketch in the space below to reflect on that impact.

Conversation Ready
Identify one or two things to share with your family and write them down in the space below.

_____

_____

_____

_____

Worship

Honor. Reverence. Praise. Devotion. Dedication. Worship is both personal and corporate. You do it on your own and with others. It is thought and action. It is moments and lifestyle. It involves your heart, mind, soul, and body. Ponder the passages below about worship. Write down some of your reflections, and then delve into the practicality of what it means to worship.

Romans 12:1–2

Psalm 95:1–7

What thoughts, reactions, or responses do those passages of Scripture stir in your heart?

_____

_____

_____

List some of the specific worship actions described in the passages above.

_____

_____

_____

Romans 12:1–2 talks about presenting your body as a living and holy sacrifice and being transformed by the renewing of your mind. How do you do that? How does that apply or how is that relevant to Sunday worship at a church?

_____

_____

_____

Study the following passages to discover how the Bible elaborates on and illuminates worship. Write down your observations from the passage. Be specific on the attitude, action, and any frequency described. Note whether the verse indicates it is something to be done individually, in a group as corporate worship, or both.

Ephesians 5:1: _____

Ephesians 5:15: _____

Ephesians 5:18–21: _____

John 4:23–24: _____

Colossians 1:1–2ff: _____

Acts 20:7: _____

Write down ways you currently worship God, both individually and as a family.

_____

_____

_____

Reflection Moment

Describe how you see the mindset of worship in your life on Sundays. In the middle of living life? On every day of the week? What can be different, better, or deeper? How does this fit with Sunday games (or practices) and travel sports? Write, draw, or sketch in the space below to symbolize your reflection moment.

Conversation Ready

Identify key points from your reflection moment and who you will share those thoughts with.

_____

_____

_____

_____

_____

Sunday Services

After studying the words "meet," "church," "building," and "worship," there is even more to be gleaned by looking at the phrase "Sunday services" relative to the question: "Sanctuary Required?" So, what about Sunday services, and does a Christian have to be in a church building sanctuary every weekend to meet for a worship service with other Christians?

Creation accounts in the Bible (Genesis 1:1–31; 2:1–3) mention only a positional ordering of days—first, second, third, fourth, fifth, sixth, seventh—not the proper noun names (Sunday, Monday, Tuesday, Wednesday, etc.) that we refer to today. Sunday, as we know it today, for Christians, has its roots in being referred to in the Bible as the "first day" and the "Lord's Day." While the term "Sabbath" is often used interchangeably or synonymously with "Sunday," the two days are distinctly different. Look up the following references to the Sabbath and fill in the chart below.

APPENDIX C

	Day Number	Name	What God Completed	What God Did	Instructions Given to Believers
Genesis 2:1–3					
Exodus 20:8					
Exodus 20:11					
Exodus 34:21					

If the topic of the Sabbath now intrigues you, an in-depth study of the topic is a worthwhile one for everyone (including travel sports families), but for this particular journey and study, our focus now turns back to Sunday.

In each of the sentences below, fill in the blanks with the words used to describe Sunday and the significant events happening that day.

Mary and Mary Magdalene came to Jesus' _____ in the early hours of the _____ day of the week. (Matthew 28:1; Mark 16:1–2; John 20:1)

Mary, Mary Magdalene, and Jesus' disciples _____ Christ on the first day of the week. (Matthew 28:8–10)

Jesus was in the _____ of the disciples after his resurrection in the evening of the _____ day to comfort and encourage them. (John 20:19–21)

People _____ to hear Paul talk (preach) and break _____ together on the _____ day of the week. (Acts 20:7)

The connection to the first day being Sunday comes in a couple of ways; the Sabbath is a common thread. The verses above mention the first day coming after the Sabbath. The Bible's creation account (Genesis 1:1–31; 2:1–3) indicates that the Sabbath is the seventh and last day of the week. The Sabbath day of the week was what we know today as Saturday, which then places what we know today as Sunday as the first day.

"In Orthodox Judaism, the Sabbath begins at sundown on Friday and ends at sundown on Saturday," Rosenfeld says. "The Jewish leaders wanted to be able to bury Christ before the Sabbath began."

And that is the second connection—the timing of Jesus' death, burial, and resurrection. Since the Sabbath was Saturday, and the Jewish people needed to make sure Jesus was not on the cross when the Sabbath began, the crucifixion took place on Friday. Crucified on Friday, the Bible tells us Christ would rise on the third day (Matthew 20:17–19; Mark 8:31; Luke 24:44–49). And that resurrection day? It is the day we know of today as Sunday, and the day the Bible refers to as the first day (Mark 16:1–2; 1 Corinthians 15:3–8).

Revelation 1:10 refers to the first day by another name—the "Lord's Day"—the day we call Sunday. The verse itself doesn't elaborate on the term, and there aren't any other references to the "Lord's Day" in the Bible. However, theologians and historians believe that Sunday is the "Lord's Day" because it is when Christ was resurrected.

Acts 20:7 is generally believed to be a description from Luke of an early worship service. It is not a scripted, detailed commandment of exactly what to do every time a group of Christians gathers—simply a glimpse into what was happening from the eyes of Luke, one of the twelve disciples. While the verse only mentions the breaking of bread and Paul speaking, it is part of the body of Scripture verses (many of which you've looked at in this study) that give guidance and inspiration to the depth and breadth of worship gatherings and services. Acts 20:7 and the surrounding verses in Acts 20:1–16 are also where the idea of preaching as we know it today comes from.

"The idea of preaching is speaking for a crowd, a corporate gathering," Rosenfeld says. "Unlike interactive dialogue and teaching with smaller groups as it was done in synagogues and temples, preaching is more of a one-way communication to a large group." Another term you'll find in commentaries describing the teaching in these particular verses and setting is "discourse" or "sermon." After speaking, Paul may or may not have answered questions from those who had gathered; the verses in Acts 20 don't tell us either way.

To review, list the things you discovered that happened on the first day of the week.

_____

_____

_____

_____

Describe the significance of the first day of the week, Sunday, also known as the Lord's Day, in your own words.

_____

_____

_____

_____

Reflection Moment

How can someone honor God and delight in Him, especially on Sundays? How do Sunday games (or practices) and travel sports participation impact that? Brainstorm ways to honor and delight in God on Sundays, both with and without sports commitments. Write, draw, or sketch in the space below to symbolize your thoughts.

Conversation Ready

Write down key reflections from this section to share with a family member. Invite a discussion. Make a plan (time/day/date) to talk and take action.

_____

_____

_____

_____

Back to the Question

Having been immersed in the details of studying words, now it's time to go back to the broader question. Take a few minutes to allow for reflection and processing before rushing onto the next part of this journey. "Sanctuary Required?" Do I have to be in a church building sanctuary every weekend to meet for a worship service with other Christians? Use the space below to write, draw, or sketch the ideas, thoughts, feelings, and responses that are stirring in your heart and soul so far.

~ Considering Life ~

We've taken our time traveling through the rich, luscious, beautiful foliage of Bible verses and made some rest stops along the way to reflect and process. That's the backdrop to the rest of this discovery journey as we travel onward, lingering in a few scenic pull-outs along the way to ponder the parts of life that impact the question, "Sanctuary Required?"

The question prompts in this section fall into three major categories: family, your athlete, and your faith community. Within those categories, the prompts cover a range of areas—and they are not all specifically about Sunday, attending services, or even travel sports. Of a reflective nature, they are all part of responding to what, in today's culture, is not as easy a question as it used to be. There is space below to jot down your thoughts, or you may want to use a personal journal.

Your Family
Think about what your life encompasses now relative to children; jobs, careers, volunteering, community involvement; personal goals, hopes, and dreams; health; and extended family. What season of life are you in as a family? Remember, the family includes you, so make sure to think about yourself here even as you think about others.

Existing Commitments
➤ What would family members give up with travel sports and/or Sunday play?

➤ What would family members be able to keep doing with travel sports and/or Sunday play?

➤ What are considered "must-do's" for your family members individually and as a family unit?

The Family Unit
➤ What are the ages of your children and who is living at home?

➤ Where does your player fall—oldest, youngest, in the middle?

➤ Are there young children, children with special needs, or extended family members who require a lot of attention or medical care?

➤ Do you or your spouse have job responsibilities that require you to work on the weekends in addition to weekday hours?

➤ How does travel sports or playing on Sundays help or hinder your family's goals, hopes, and dreams?

Your Player

Passion. Interests. Dreams. From the beginning, that is what it has been all about as you've watched your athlete's love for the sport. And you've been thankful for the opportunities that have come and have loved watching your athlete thrive. And so, decisions regarding travel sports and Sunday play are nuanced by wanting to do all you can for your kids—giving them most and best opportunities possible. Yet, there is also a time and a season for everything (Ecclesiastes 3:1–8).

Is travel sports and Sunday play necessary for your player, and important *now*, in this season and time of life? Work through the question prompts below to reflect on this. Much like admissions counselors suggest when students include their habits and preferences on college dorm applications for roommate matching, be as honest and realistic as possible in your reflection as you consider things as they are, not as you wish they were.

Practical Considerations

➤ What is the age of your player?

➤ How close is your player to graduation from high school?

➤ What time would any Sunday games or practices be?

➤ Is this a year-round team with year-round Sunday commitments?

➤ Are there other organization or team options that don't involve Sunday play that would be viable options for your athlete's interest and skill level?

Dreams and Goals

➤ If your son or daughter is a high schooler, what hopes and dreams does he or she have for after high school?

➤ What character, abilities, and capabilities do you want to see your player develop over the next year, three years, or five years?

➤ What is crucial in how your son or daughter spends Sunday right now (relative to age, maturity level, and character development)?

➤ If your athlete is in high school, is the sport (and travel sports in general) still enjoyable? Is there interest in continuing to play after high school, whether on a college-level or through some other avenue? Does your athlete have an equal desire to pursue an area of study, degree, or career?

This next set of question prompts is about areas not often considered. Think for a moment about jobs that involve shift hours or expect weekend travel for business appointments or conferences. Think about hobbies or community work that require time investments on the weekend. Maybe that is even the situation for you, your spouse, or your kids' grandparents.

➤ How do adults keep their faith strong in those circumstances?

➤ How do adults worship as part of a group of believers in a service that's held in a building on the weekends if they have weekend jobs or work travel commitments?

➤ What is the difference between what adults do in the name of jobs, hobbies, or community work and what your son or daughter wants to do in the name of the sports?

➤ If your son or daughter is seriously looking at playing competitively beyond high school, is it time to use travel sports as a tool to help teach foundational life skills for a potential future schedule? One that could be heavy with travel and likely include a variety of influences, choices, and weekday and weekend commitments?

➤ Is your player ready for that?

➤ Is your family ready for that?

➤ Is it too early?

➤ If your player has siblings, what examples and foundations are still needed for everyone?

Your Faith Community

It's easy to sit in a pew, gather for a small group Bible study, meet in gatherings of fellowship, and listen to sermons week after week, month after month, and year after year without really realizing how important your faith community is in the fabric of your life. It's also easy to make assumptions or presumptions without really taking the time to examine the actual documented core beliefs behind what you think you are hearing in your faith community.

The following set of questions is not designed to foster rebelliousness, self-righteousness, or argumentativeness about the leadership or ways of your faith community, but instead for you to have a clear understanding of what you may have just assumed or taken for granted. And you may be surprised. While what you find may confirm what you already know, you may also find that some things are not quite as firm as you thought or maybe even entirely different.

➤ What is the teaching in your faith community about Saturdays and Sundays? (Reflect and jot down what you think to be the teaching and then do the research to determine the reality—look at church doctrinal statements, talk to church leaders, etc.)

➤ What happens in your faith community on Saturdays and Sundays (any special gatherings, services, traditions, or commitments)?

➤ What meetings, gatherings, or services (Saturday, Sunday, or otherwise) are "must-do's" for everyone (including you and your family) in your faith community?

Connecting Truths

It's time to look back through the pages of this study and find your own family's story. Much like capturing many moments in a single photo album or scrapbook, now it is time to connect all that you've studied, discovered, and reflected on regarding the question of "Sanctuary Required?" For some, this part of your story will come quickly and easily. For others, it may simply be about making the best choice right now that allows you to take the next step in life and on the travel sports journey wherever that choice leads—remembering that adventures rarely go in a straight line. Unexpected road turns, mountain treks, valley terrain, and scenic pull-outs may let you know that it is time to chart a new course—and that's OK. For our family, the decision for travelball and Sunday play was a process, and one that occurred over time.

Write down some of the key ideas and concepts that have stood out to you from this study.

_____

_____

_____

Note some of the verses that have stood out to you from this study and why.

_____

_____

_____

Write down new thoughts that this study brought up that you hadn't thought about before.

_____

_____

_____

Look back at the presuppositions you started with. Do any of your beliefs need to be changed or discarded? Are there any that you can keep? Write those thoughts here.

_____

_____

_____

After doing this study, what thoughts come to mind about playing sports on Sunday and Sunday worship services?

_____

_____

_____

Reflection Moment

Circle back to Hebrews 10:23–25, Psalm 95:1–7, and Acts 2:42–47. How do you carry out these principles of Scripture if you *don't* play travel sports and Sunday ball? How do you carry out these principles of Scripture if you *do* play travel sports and Sunday ball? Write, draw, or sketch your thoughts in the space below.

Conversation Ready

Think about who you want to share your discoveries and thoughts with. Write down key areas to share in the space below. Remember, hold all this loosely as you share. You have spent a lot of time thinking and pondering, while the people you are sharing with probably haven't. Give grace to people as you speak. Give them time to process, reflect, and make decisions with you. Let them catch up to what you are thinking and to your ideas and opinions. Make this a springboard discussion to discover even more so you can reach decisions together, whether that happens quickly or takes a few days. And while there may be a deadline associated with some decisions, as much as possible let there be time for the process and processing.

A special thank you to David Rosenfeld for his contributions on church history and theology throughout this study. Dave holds undergraduate and graduate degrees, including a master of divinity and a master of sacred theology. He served as a pastor for several years following graduation. Dave has been an avid baseball fan all his life, playing baseball in Little League® and cheering on the Chicago Cubs. In 2014, Dave co-founded and led the first homeschool high school baseball team in Illinois as the team's assistant head coach. In 2017, he took on the role of baseball athletic director for the team. Dave and his wife Sue Rosenfeld, author of this book, On the Road for Travelball: A Parent's Guide to Traveling the Travel Team Circuit without *Constantly* Blowing a Circuit, *have three boys who were involved in various youth and college sports, including travel baseball.*

Appendix D
Baseball Trivia Smorgasbord

- The distance between the pitcher's mound and home plate is 60 feet, 6 inches.[1]

- The pitcher's mound has a diameter of 18 feet[2] and is 10 inches high.[3]

- The odds of a Major League Baseball player being caught while attempting to steal a base is 3 in 10.[4]

- The odds of a Major League Baseball fan catching a foul ball is 1 in 563.[5]

- George A. Baird, an inventor from Chicago, developed an electric baseball scoreboard in 1908.[6]

- Fenway Park's 1934 scoreboard included Morse code of the team's former owners' initials.[7]

- Before Kauffman Stadium in Kansas City was renovated in 2007, the Royals had a crown-shaped centerfield scoreboard.[8]

- Before Herschel Greer Stadium was demolished, the Nashville Sounds had a guitar-shaped scoreboard.[9]

- The Wrigley Field scoreboard in Chicago is 27 feet high by 75 feet wide, and the top is 60 feet above the ground.[10]

- Only two stadiums—Wrigley Field and Fenway Park—have vintage manual scoreboards.[11]

- Wrigley Field is the oldest ballpark in the National League.[12]

- Architect Zachary Taylor Davis designed Wrigley Field and Comiskey Park.[13]

- Singing the National Anthem before every game began at Wrigley.[14]

- From 1903–1968, pitcher mounds were 15 inches high.[15]

- In 1869, ball players' bats were different sizes and shapes; however, rule refinements that same year included the regulation that set the maximum bat length at 42 inches.[16]

- Legends swirl around whether Pete Browning, Arlie Latham, or Gus Weyhing first swung a Louisville Slugger bat.[17]

- The original name of the Louisville Slugger bat was "the Falls City Slugger in reference to Louisville's location at the falls of the Ohio River."[18]

- By 1933, the Louisville Slugger company was selling golf clubs in addition to bats, and in 1966, the company bought Wally Enterprises of Canada (a sporting goods company) and rebranded the hockey sticks as Louisville TPS (Tournament Player Series).[19]

- Taking a base on balls started at 9 balls and gradually decreased until 1889 when it was reduced to 4 balls, as it is today.[20]

- Louisville Slugger Factory's branding machine that "stamps 'Louisville Slugger' and the player's signature on each personalized bat" is heated to 1,400 degrees.[21]

- Ted Williams was "known by nicknames including 'the Kid,' 'the Thumper,' and 'the Splendid Splinter.'"[22]

- Baseball gloves became mandatory in the mid-1880s.[23]

- The legendary Louisville Slugger wooden bat trademark name was registered in 1894 by Bud Hillerich.[24]

- "The metal baseball bat was first patented in the 1920s."[25]

- The average price of a Major League Baseball concession stand hot dog was $4.95 in 2019.[26]

Notes

Chapter 1
1. https://www.baseball-reference.com/bullpen/Pitcher's_mound.
2. Kevin Hile, "Weather Fundamentals," *The Handy Weather Answer Book, Second Edition* (Canton, MI: Visible Ink Press, 2009), 17.
3. https://encyclopedia.thefreedictionary.com/on+deck.
4. Chris Landers, "Discover the mysterious origins of some of baseball's most well-known terms," July 13, 2017, https://www.mlb.com/cut4/more-wacky-stories-behind-baseball-terms-c218978328.

Chapter 2
1. Jimmy Stamp, "The Pay Phone's Journey from Patent to Urban Relic," September 18, 2014, smithsonianmag.com/history/first-and-last-pay-phone-180952727.
2. Associated Press, "Left-field pole named after Fisk, historic HR," June 13, 2005, https://www.espn.com/mlb/news/story?id=2084485.
3. Jimmy Stamp, "The Invention of the Baseball Mitt," July 16, 2013, smithsonianmag.com/arts-culture/the-invention-of-the-baseball-mitt-12799848/.

Chapter 3
1. Alex Daniel, "40 Facts About Words That Will Blow Your Mind," February 20, 2020, https://bestlifeonline.com/word-facts.
2. "Sunflower Seeds: Ideal as a Snack and an Ingredient," Nutritional Power of Sunflower Seeds Newsletter, vol. 2.1, http://www.sunflowernsa.com/uploads/4/nusun_factsheet_vol_2.1.pdf.
3. National Sunflower Association, https://www.sunflowernsa.com/all-about/faq/#8.
4. "William A. Bentley: Pioneering Photographer of Snowflakes," https://siarchives.si.edu/history/featured-topics/stories/wilson-bentley-pioneering-photographer-snowflakes.
5. M. Shahbandeh, "Luggage cases: UK manufacturers' sales volume 2008–2020," August 12, 2021, https:/www.statista.com/statistics/468715/luggage-cases-manufacturers-sales-volume-united-kingdom-uk.
6. M. Shahbandeh, "Travel goods unit sales in the U.S. 2003–2019," November 23, 2020, https:/www.statista.com/statistics/441906/number-of-travel-goods-sold-in-the-us-by-category.
7. Stacey Platt, *What's a Disorganized Person to Do?* (Artisan, 2010), 254, 255, 138.

Chapter 4

1. *Guinness World Records 2017* (London, United Kingdom: Guinness World Records Limited, 2016), 101.
2. Alex Daniel, "40 Facts About Words That Will Blow Your Mind," February 20, 2020, https://bestlifeonline.com/word-facts.
3. Danielle S. Hammelef, "What are the Odds?" *The Old Farmer's Almanac 2015*, (Dublin, NH: Yankee Publishing Incorporated, 2014), 182–186.
4. Caroline Picard, "35 Coolest Random Pieces of Trivia That Will Impress Your Friends," December 27, 2019, https://www.goodhousekeeping.com/life/g25692093/random-trivia/?slide=24.
5. Monica M. Smith, "Lincoln Logs Inventor John Lloyd Wright," August 23, 2018, https://invention.si.edu/lincoln-logs-inventor-john-lloyd-wright.
6. "Lincoln Logs," https://www.toyhalloffame.org/toys/lincoln-logs.

Chapter 5

1. *Guinness World Records 2017* (London, United Kingdom: Guinness World Records Limited, 2016), "Largest Collection of Sunglasses," 92.
2. Kevin Hile, "Clouds and Precipitation," *The Handy Weather Answer Book, Second Edition* (Canton, MI: Visible Ink Press, 2009), 92.
3. Ibid., "Clouds and Precipitation," 93.
4. Ibid., "Weather Fundamentals," 12.

Chapter 6

1. *Guinness World Records 2017* (London, United Kingdom: Guinness World Records Limited, 2016), "Heaviest Strawberry," 89.
2. Ibid., "Longest . . . Cucumber," 89.
3. Ibid., "Heaviest . . . Watermelon," 88.
4. Angela Weight, "Smart and Tasty Snack Ideas for the Ball Field," February 24, 2016, https://travelballparents.com/?s=snack+ideas+for+the+ball+field.
5. Angela Weight, "Ballpark Meals to Fill Them Up, Not Slow Them Down," March 10, 2016, https://travelballparents.com/?s=ballpark+meals.
6. *Guinness World Records 2017* (London, United Kingdom: Guinness World Records Limited, 2016), "Fast Facts," 87.

Chapter 7

1. *Are You Smarter Than a Fifth Grader?* board game (Pawtucket, RI: Hasbro and Parker Brothers, JMBP, Inc. 2007), Board Game Hasbro Games, Consumer Affairs Department, P.O. Box 200, Pawtucket, RI 02862.
2. One website that talks about state symbols, including Arkansas, is https://statesymbolsusa.org. You'll also find information about national

symbols as well as places (for example, historic buildings, landmarks, and parks) on that site. The Arkansas Tourism Official Site, at https://www.arkansas.com/, offers visitor information and free resources, including a story titled "Family Travels: Murfreesboro." And for more details about mining for diamonds at Arkansas' Crater of Diamonds State Park, go to https://www.arkansasstateparks.com/parks/crater-diamonds-state-park.

3. "Route 66 History," http://www.route66world.com/66_history.

4. An interesting May 2018 online article, "Why GPS will never make the road atlas obsolete" (https://nypost.com/2018/05/26/why-gps-will-never-make-the-road-atlas-obsolete) by Erik Spitznagel includes fun anecdotes from Rand McNally road atlas fans. Rand McNally didn't start with road atlases though, and historical company information can be found at the "Rand McNally & Co." entry in the online Encyclopedia of Chicago (http://www.encyclopedia.chicagohistory.org/pages/2823.html) and on the company's website (https://www.randmcnally.com/retrospective). Today, Rand McNally produces and publishes much more than road atlases. Things of note on the Rand McNally website are the "Rand McNally Road Atlases Retrospective," a pictorial journey of atlas covers, and a company timeline on the "Our History" page of the website (https://www.randmcnally.com/about/history).

5. "First race held at the Indianapolis Motor Speedway," https://www.history.com/this-day-in-history/first-race-is-held-at-the-indianapolis-motor-speedway.

6. Of note on the IMS website (https://www.indianapolismotorspeedway.com) is the availability of "Indianapolis 500 Radio Broadcasts" for purchase, and a dynamic digital library archive featuring photos, quotes, articles, and audio. The speedway grounds include a museum open to the public and track tours. There is a fee for both the museum and tours.

Chapter 8

1. "What Is Braille?" https://www.afb.org/blindness-and-low-vision/braille/what-braille.

2. Brandon Specktor, "What Is the Longest Word in English? Hint: It's 189,819 Letters Long," July 16, 2021, https://www.rd.com/article/longest-word-english.

3. Arlene Miller, "Language Trivia: 25 More Fun Facts," June 29, 2018, https://bigwords101.com/2018/blog/language-trivia-25-more-fun-facts.

4. Freundt, Johanna K., and Wolfgang A. Linke. "Titin as a Force-Generating Muscle Protein under Regulatory Control." Applied Journal of Physiology.

American Physiological Society, May 16, 2019, https://journals.
physiology.org/doi/full/10.1152/japplphysiol.00865.2018.

5. Herzog, Walter, "The multiple roles of titin in muscle contraction and force production." *Biophysical reviews* vol. 10,4 (2018): 1187–1199. doi:10.1007/s12551-017-0395-y, https://pubmed.ncbi.nlm.nih. gov/29353351/.

6. *Are You Smarter Than a Fifth Grader?* board game (Pawtucket, RI: Hasbro and Parker Brothers, JMBP, Inc. 2007), Board Game Hasbro Games, Consumer Affairs Department, P.O. Box 200, Pawtucket, RI 02862.

7. Ibid.

8. Alex Daniel, "40 Facts About Words That Will Blow Your Mind," February 20, 2020, https://bestlifeonline.com/word-facts.

9. Captain Bob Figular, "Safe Boat Operations – Boat Nomenclature and Terminology," https://americanboating.org/safety_nomenclature.asp.

10. National Oceanic and Atmospheric Administration (NOA), "Why do Ships use 'port' and 'starboard' instead of 'left' and 'right'?", National Ocean Service Website, February 26, 2021, https://oceanservice.noaa. gov/facts/port-starboard.html.

Chapter 9

1. John D. Morris, "Hymn 27 Christ the Lord Is Risen Today," *How Firm a Foundation in Scripture & Song*, (Green Forest, AZ: Master Books, 1999), 240.

2. Matthew 14:13–21; Mark 6:31–44; Luke 9:12–17; John 6:1–14.

3. Joni Eareckson Tada, John MacArthur, and Robert and Bobbie Wolgemuth, "Introduction," *O Worship the King*, (Wheaton, IL: Lane T. Dennis, Ph.D., Crossway Books, 2000), 11.

Chapter 10

1. Kate Silzer, "The staying power of the smiley face," August 15, 2019, https://www.artsy.net/article/artsy-editorial-staying-power-smiley-face.

2. Jimmy Stamp, "The Pay Phone's Journey from Patent to Urban Relic," September 18, 2014, https://www.smithsonianmag.com/history/first-and-last-pay-phone-180952727.

3. https://www.encyclopedia.com/science-and-technology/computers-and-electrical-engineering/electrical-engineering/telephone-booth.

4. WBIR staff, "865 'VOL' area code assignment was clever keypad kiss-up," November 19, 2014, https://www.wbir.com/article/news/local/865-vol-area-code-assignment-was-clever-keypad-kiss-up/94855247.

5. Greg Pallone, "Here's How the '321' Space Coast Area Code was Born," October 31, 2019, https://www.mynews13.com/fl/orlando/

news/2019/10/31/here-s-how-the--321--space-coast-area-code-was-
born. Pallone's article highlights his fun conversations with Ozzie
Osband, a resident of Titusville, Florida, who launched a petition to
present to the Florida Public Service Commission.

Chapter 11

1. https://www.nps.gov/subjects/nationalregister/database-research.
   htm#table. *The Boston Globe* highlighted Fenway Park's National
   Register status in its article "Fenway Park added to National Register
   of Historic Places" by Martin Finucane on March 7, 2012. Historical
   information and interesting anecdotes about Fenway Park can be found
   at the Boston Preservation Alliance's website, https://www.boston
   preservation.org/advocacy-project/fenway-park.
2. Jordan Bastian, "Wrigley named National Historic Landmark," November
   19, 2020, https://www.mlb.com/news/wrigley-field-national-historic-
   landmark.
3. https://www.nps.gov/subjects/nationalregister/database-research.
   htm#table.
4. National Oceanic and Atmospheric Administration (NOA), "What are
   barnacles?", National Ocean Service Website, February 26, 2021,
   https://oceanservice.noaa.gov/facts/barnacles.html.
5. A Public Broadcasting Service (PBS) production and broadcast, the "A
   Capitol Fourth" concert celebrated its 40th anniversary in 2020. While
   the 2020 concert was virtual because of the COVID-19 pandemic, the
   concert traditionally took place on the Capitol grounds with a main
   stage and several smaller ones. Backdropped by the Washington Mon-
   ument and Mall, the main stage faced the Capitol. In addition to its
   history of an in-person audience, the show is broadcast for viewers
   across the country and in the military. According to the website, multiple cameras are positioned around Washington for viewers to get
   the best streaming experience. Learn more about the concert, July 4
   history, and fireworks at https://www.pbs.org/a-capitol-fourth.
6. Alex Daniel, "40 Facts About Words That Will Blow Your Mind," February
   20, 2020, https://bestlifeonline.com/word-facts.

Chapter 12

1. Inducted into the National Toy Hall of Fame in 2017 and part of a 2018
   White House "Made in America Product Showcase," check out the Wiffle
   ball's company site to learn more about the company's history and the
   rules of the game at http://www.wiffle.com. There are also a couple
   of Wiffle ball-related National Public Radio (NPR) resources at npr.org,

including "Wiffle Ball at 50," by Linda Wertheimer, August 23, 2003, https://www.npr.org/templates/story/story.php?storyId=1405993, and "Wiffle Ball: Born and Still Made in the USA," Chris Arnold, September 5, 2011, https://www.npr.org/2011/09/05/140145711/wiffle-ball-born-and-still-made-in-the-usa.
2. A classic, the Wiffle ball had 1953 origins in retired semi-pro pitcher David Nelson Mullany's backyard. "Wiffle Ball: Born and Still Made in the USA," Chris Arnold, September 5, 2011, https://www.npr.org/2011/09/05/140145711/wiffle-ball-born-and-still-made-in-the-usa.
3. Debra Fine, *The Fine Art of Small Talk: How to Start a Conversation, Keep It Going, Build Networking Skills—and Leave a Positive Impression!* (New York, NY: Hyperion, 2005).
4. "Where Does 'Hello' Come From?" https://www.merriam-webster.com/words-at-play/the-origin-of-hello.
5. Alex Daniel, "40 Facts About Words That Will Blow Your Mind," February 20, 2020. https://bestlifeonline.com/word-facts.
6. https://www.etymonline.com/word/good-bye.

Chapter 13
1. Danielle S. Hammelef, "What are the Odds?", *The Old Farmer's Almanac 2015* (Dublin, NH: Yankee Publishing Incorporated, 2014), 182–186.
2. Ibid.
3. Ron Filipkowski, *Travelball: How to Start and Manage a Successful Travel Baseball Team*, "Chapter 20: Managing Parents" (Sarasota, FL: Harmonic Research Associates, 2011), 293–294.
4. Ibid.
5. Danielle S. Hammelef, "What are the Odds?", *The Old Farmer's Almanac 2015* (Dublin, NH: Yankee Publishing Incorporated, 2014), 182–186.

Chapter 14
1. For design and color enthusiasts, one shade of blue was Pantone's Color of the Year in 2020. Learn more at https://www.pantone.com.
2. http://www.nebraskatrackofficials.org/officials.html.
3. Bill Severns, *Keepers of the Sandlot: Coaching, Parenting and Playing for Keeps!* (Keepers of the Sandlot, 2009), 96.
4. Bill Severns, "Give Up What's Holding You Back," November 19, 2019, https://www.keeperslegacy.org/blog/2019/11/19/give-up-whats-holding-you-back.
5. https://www.nfhs.org/media/869198/nfhs-hockey-brochure.pdf.
6. https://www.sayyestoofficiating.com/become-a-sports-official/sports/volleyball.

Chapter 15

1. Martie Majoros, "Beauty on a Budget," *The Old Farmer's Almanac 2015* (Dublin, NH: Yankee Publishing Incorporated, 2014), 188–192.
2. United States Department of Transportation Bureau of Transportation Statistics, table 1-04, https://www.bts.gov/content/public-road-and-street-mileage-united-states-type-surfacea.
3. "Most pull ups in 24 hours (female)," https://www.guinnessworldrecords.com/world-records/103859-most-pull-ups-in-24-hours-female.
4. "Most pull ups in 24 hours (male)," https://www.guinnessworldrecords.com/world-records/most-pull-ups-in-24-hours.
5. "National Doughnut Day," https://nationaldaycalendar.com/national-doughnut-day-first-friday-in-june/.
6. "National Doughnut Day," https://nationaldaycalendar.com/national-doughnut-day-november-5.

Special Interview Feature: Behind the Scenes at Wrigley Field with Organist Gary Pressy

1. http://mlb.mlb.com/chc/ballpark/information/index.jsp?content=history.
2. https://www.mlb.com/cubs/ballpark/information/guide.
3. "April 26, 1941: Cubs are first MLB team to have organ music," April 26, 2016, https://www.chicagotribune.com/sports/cubs/ct-wrigley-field-organ-music-archive-20160419-story.html.

Appendix D: Baseball Trivia

1. https://www.mlb.com/official-information/basics/field.
2. https://www.mlb.com/glossary/rules/field-dimensions.
3. https://www.baseball-reference.com/bullpen/Pitcher's_mound.
4. Danielle S. Hammelef, "What are the Odds?" *The Old Farmer's Almanac 2015* (Dublin, NH: Yankee Publishing Incorporated, 2014), 182–186.
5. Ibid.
6. Scott Allen, "100 Years of Scoreboard Watching," June 21, 2010, http://mentalfloss.com/article/24976/100-years-scoreboard-watching.
7. Ibid.
8. Ibid.
9. Ibid.
10. David Schaper, "Inside Wrigley Field, The Scorekeepers Stay True to Baseball's Beginnings." August 12, 2017, https://www.npr.org/2017/08/12/542585335/inside-wrigley-field-the-scorekeepers-stay-true-to-baseballs-beginnings.

11. Ibid.
12. Derek Miller, http://baseball.derekmiller.us/wrigley.php.
13. Ibid.
14. Ibid.
15. https://www.baseball-reference.com/bullpen/Pitcher's_mound.
16. David Magee and Philip Shirley, *Sweet Spot: 125 Years of Baseball and the Louisville Slugger* (Chicago, IL: Triumph Books, 2009), 5, 8.
17. Ibid., 11, 14, 15.
18. Ibid., 15.
19. Ibid., 54, 83.
20. Ibid., 22.
21. Ibid., 134.
22. Ibid., 68.
23. Ibid., 8.
24. Ibid., 15.
25. Ibid., 96.
26. "Average concession stand prices in Major League Baseball from 2010 to 2016 (in U.S. dollars)," https://www.statista.com/statistics/202619/concession-stand-prices-in-mlb.

On the Road for Travelball

A Parent's Guide to
Traveling the Travel Team Circuit
without *Constantly* Blowing a Circuit

SUE ROSENFELD

Additional copies of

On the Road for Travelball:
A Parent's Guide to Traveling the Travel Team Circuit
without Constantly *Blowing a Circuit*

can be ordered at Amazon.com.

For bulk orders, or to book Sue Rosenfeld to speak,
contact Sue directly at
OntheRoadforTravelball@gmail.com

Index

W

Y

CPSIA information can be obtained
at www.ICGtesting.com
Printed in the USA
BVHW030035301022
650620BV00006B/121